THE ELDER

THE ELDER

BY

DR. MARC B. COOPER
JAMES C. SELMAN

The Eldering Institute
Bainbridge, Washington

THE ELDER

Published by Sahalie Press
Woodinville, Washington

ISBN: 978-0-9763584-4-2

Library of Congress Control Number: 2010941988

Printed in the U.S.A.

First Edition, 2011

Editing by Matt King and Shae Hadden

Book design by Lightbourne, Inc.

ACKNOWLEDGEMENTS

This book has two authors on the cover, but we certainly didn't create this book alone. Our special thanks go out to: Chris Creamer, who guided the process from beginning to end; Shae Hadden, who kept us on message and was instrumental in the revision process; Matt King, who continues to amaze with his attention to story line and character development; Sharon Knoll, for her ever-valuable feedback..

We'd also like to thank the many volunteers and participants of the Eldering Institute®, our community of Elders who have made it their purpose to transform the story of aging from one of loss, disappointment and decline to one of possibility, mastery and purpose. You are instrumental in our mission to build programs and resources to spread the word of wisdom in action.

To all Elders who empower others to determine their own journey and find their own path to a purposeful and fulfilling life, we thank you.

Dr. Marc B. Cooper

James C. Selman

INTRODUCTION

Ours is the later, last wisdom of the afternoon.

We know that love, like light, grows dearer
toward the dark.

—Archibald MacLeish

IN 1990, THERE WERE 32 MILLION PEOPLE IN
the U.S. aged 65 and older. There will be 72 million people over
65 by the year 2020. And by 2050, one in every five Americans
will be over 65.

The phenomenon of a rapidly aging population is one of
the most significant global developments of the 21st Century. By
2047, the number of people aged 60 and over on the entire planet
will outnumber people under 15 for the first time in human his-
tory. What will this mean to us personally and socially?

We at The Eldering Institute are working on designing a
future where the latter years of one's life are about interdepen-
dence—a future in which each of us can experience the satisfaction of 'being known' and 'being valued' for who we are.

Our mission, and the intention of this book, is to demonstrate the possibility of growing older with vitality and inspiration. That's what The Eldering Institute is all about: *making the
rest of your life be the best of your life.*

The book is written as a fable and the message is that
new possibilities exist for aging. What if aging wasn't a prison

sentence, but an authentic opportunity? What if aging was something to look forward to rather than dread? What if aging was a transition to joy, peace of mind, vitality and self-expression? What if those qualities that come with age and experience—wisdom, kindness, and love—governed the world? What then?

Dr. Marc B. Cooper

James C. Selman

FOREWORD

*Summary of Keynote Speech given at the David Suzuki Foundation
Elders Forum 2009 in Vancouver, Canada*

"Our Elders are our knowledge-keepers. We look to them for Wisdom, Guidance and Validation. Guidance when we face the huge challenges that life puts in front of us. Validation when we must do what we believe is right—especially when others cannot understand or cannot see what we see. We depend on them for Wisdom, the perspective that only they can have that distills all the knowledge and experience they have gained from living. We depend on them to pass that wisdom on from generation to generation.

Being an Elder is not about age. You don't become an Elder because you've grown old.

To me, an Elder is someone whose integrity I trust and whose wisdom I respect. That trust and respect must be earned to be real.

Our culture is based on respect. We value respect that is earned. The trust you acquire, the standing you have in your community, is earned by living with integrity—by sharing your wisdom with words and demonstrating it with your actions.

Talk is good. Actions are stronger.

We need what our Elders bring forward."

Kilsli Kaji Sting

Miles G. Richardson

Former President of the Haida Nation
Former Chief Commissioner of the British Columbia Treaty Commission
Board of Directors, The David Suzuki Foundation
Officer of the Order of Canada

CONTENTS

Come to the Edge

Come to the edge.
 We might fall.
Come to the edge.
 It's too high!
COME TO THE EDGE!
 And they came,
 and he pushed,
 and they flew.

—CHRISTOPHER LOGUE

PROLOGUE

AT JUST PAST SEVEN ON A COLD AND RAINY February evening, Samuel Block looked back over his shoulder as he missed the exit off Interstate 405. He cursed loudly, knowing he'd just added another ten minutes to an already long, tedious drive from South Seattle. That was the way his entire day had gone. Unfocused. Samuel had drifted between reveries and worries all day long, feeling lost and out of sorts.

Tomorrow was his birthday. He'd be turning 65. It didn't seem possible. How had so many years passed so quickly? What had happened to all his dreams?

Like so many of his fellow Boomers, he had once felt the future held so much promise. He'd believed they were the generation ordained to change the world, and in his youth, the world had seemed his oyster. But now, on the very verge of turning 65, life seemed to be serving him frozen fish sticks.

That thought had hit him hard earlier when he'd taken a good look in the bathroom mirror. It revealed what his mind could not accept. He was growing old. He held an image in his mind of what he looked like—but the ever-objective mirror showed him it was 20 years out of date.

All day his mind had been spinning. Retirement age. Time to grab the brass ring and step off the merry-go-round of the career carnival. Time to cash in and take it easy. Kick back and let others take the reigns, while he sailed off into the golden sunset.

Not even close. That was part of why Samuel had been so deeply distracted all day. He was supposed to be approaching retirement, but he knew he wasn't there—not by a long shot.

Samuel ran his own business: *SB Accounting & Financial Services*. He and two assistants did all the work tailored to the needs of small business owners. Samuel enjoyed the work that had provided him with a decent living for years, but now business was suffering in the sluggish economy. The whole national outlook and shaky recovery made retirement appear farther and farther away to Samuel, both mentally and fiscally.

His office had been at the same location in Redmond, Washington for almost twenty-eight years, next door to a dental practice. He and the dentist, Harry Braden, had started about the same time in the early '80s. But Harry had retired and sold his practice to a couple of younger dentists five years ago. Samuel still received periodic postcards and emails from Harry, asking when he was going to come in out of the cold and rain and join him in Prescott, Arizona for sunshine and golf.

It was dark, gloomy days like this when Samuel questioned his decision to stay in the Pacific Northwest. Maybe if he'd moved some place sunnier, everything would have turned out better. The thought of sunnier places turned his thoughts to the early days with Dorothy—they'd gotten married several years after college. Dorothy had seen him as the young business owner, a soon-to-be captain of industry with mighty aspirations. By day they'd dream about a life together full of adventure and travel and in the evenings go listen to up-and-coming rock bands in Seattle, twisting and shouting the night away. Healthy. Young. In love.

Samuel sighed. Those were good times. But Dorothy was long gone. Thirteen years ago, she'd grown restless waiting for Samuel to make it big and had become involved with another man. That had been a harsh pill to swallow. Worse than any of the many meds he now had to take.

His divorce, coupled with putting his son through college and then through a Master's program, had depleted his savings. And with the current economic climate, he didn't see any way he could stop working in the next decade. Though Samuel had developed a solid network of loyal clients, he hadn't been able to grow his business. And frankly, as a saleable asset, it was laughable. Who would buy a small accounting firm the bulk of whose clients were as old as he?

As Samuel took the next freeway off ramp and began to wind his way home through dark streets, an ominous sense of hopelessness crowded his thoughts. Just like missing the freeway exit, his life's journey seemed to have taken a wrong turn as well.

His ideal of a long and happy marriage crushed, his relationship with their only child, David, had suffered as well. They had grown apart since the bitter divorce. David had started a career and a family. And though David lived

3

less than an hour north in the town of Snohomish, Samuel seldom saw him.

To add to the heartbreak was how little time Samuel spent with Jimmy, his six-year-old grandson, whom he adored. Like leaves caught in the current of unseen eddies, he and his son and grandson traveled their own disconnected paths. Samuel felt isolated from them. He wanted to be more a part of their lives, but he didn't know how.

He knew this helpless attitude fueled a growing sense of despair which darkened his entire outlook and made the years ahead appear even bleaker. He didn't want to give into these or other gloomy thoughts like his health and financial concerns, but, tonight, he couldn't seem to shake them.

As he waited at a long traffic light, the tick-tack, tick-tack of the turn signal hypnotically transported him deeper into his murky trance. Sixty-five years old. A significant milestone. He should be celebrating. Instead, he was dreading it. The day only served to remind him that his life was not what he'd hoped. He felt like he should be more in control of his future. He should know the road ahead. His life had held promise for many years. But now he felt lost, directionless. Looking ahead, all he could see were roadblocks and hazards.

The traffic light finally turned green, but Samuel hesitated. He knew his way home, but where was he *really* going?

THE MESSAGE

SAMUEL PULLED HIS '99 CELICA INTO A TIGHT parking spot between a cement post and an SUV whose driver had ignored the "Compact Only" painted in bold letters on the parking space. Another sign of the times. People only played by the rules if it suited them. *Where was civility? Where was common sense?* It made Samuel feel even older that he valued fair play and respect. *When did values like that go out of style?*

He opened his car door carefully to prevent banging it against the concrete pillar. He couldn't afford a new car—or even a new 'used' car, for that matter. His Celica had to last a long time. He wondered what would happen when he couldn't drive anymore. Images of shabby retirement homes and assisted living apartments tumbled through his head. The enormity of the next ten to twenty years pinned him momentarily to his seat. He closed his eyes and breathed slowly. *Nothing is preordained*, he thought. *Nothing is written in stone.* He glanced in the rearview mirror, mumbling aloud, "Careful, Block, it's getting a bit dodgy when you start going all *Lawrence of Arabia* on yourself."

With a forced chuckle, Samuel regained his composure, gathered the work he'd brought home and headed to the elevator. The building was over 30 years old, built before Microsoft had moved into Redmond. Since those halcyon days, Redmond had exploded. At least housing prices had. Samuel knew he'd never be able to afford his condo nowadays.

He felt overly tired. His last appointment had taken it out of him. He'd tried to schedule the meeting in Burien earlier in the day to avoid the evening rush hour, but the owner, who operated a small video game shop, was expecting a new shipment of the latest Halo install-ment. He had told him, "I'll have kids lined up around the block...and at fifty bucks a pop, it's like harvest time on the farm. You'll have to come by after four when things slow down."

What could Samuel say? Business was business and he needed to keep his clients happy. His office phone wasn't exactly ringing off the hook with new clients and he had no chance against larger accounting firms. Plus, he was competing with software like Peachtree, Quicken and TurboTax. It seemed people should value his forty years of experience more than a piece of software. If only more people recognized him for what he was good at.

In the elevator, he pushed the fourth-floor button and leaned against the back wall, waiting for the intolerably slow door to close. Samuel knew Social Security wouldn't be enough to live on. He'd have to keep on working. And with the economy sputtering and the way the government was operating, Social Security wasn't such a sure thing.

And that was just the financial side. He had his health issues to worry about as well. Back pain, a Morton's neuroma in his right foot, a touch of arthritis in his hip and left knee, hypertension, elevated cholesterol, and prostate problems. He was taking five medications a day, some of them twice a day. All the opaque orange-brown bottles with the large white labels huddled together in his medicine cabinet looked like a micro-pharmacy. Some days it was difficult just keeping his meds straight.

That was one of his hardest challenges in staying positive: feeling healthy. He dreamed of what it would be like to be in his physical prime again. To feel able to take on the world. Like he had at first with Dorothy. His meds couldn't give him that same sense of well-being. To be physically carefree would be a birthday gift at any age.

Finally arriving at his floor, he fished in his pocket for the door key as he walked down the hall. Samuel contemplated what awaited him inside. Cold, empty rooms. Maybe a blinking light on the answering machine. He didn't get many calls. Who'd remember to wish him a happy birthday? He'd received a few birthday cards but there was no big celebration planned. Who'd plan it? Only one face came to mind and Samuel had already told his best friend, Thad, that he didn't want a party. He and Thad had made plans to mark the occasion next week over a beer and a burger.

Honestly, Samuel wasn't really sure whether he could take a celebration. Safer to be alone with his thoughts. No forced smiles or pretended joviality. Tomorrow, he'd turn 65 alone. Work all day. *Just another day in paradise,* he mused. Not quite the Margaritaville Jimmy Buffet had sung about in the '70s.

He jiggled the key in his door and unlocked it. He swiped the light switch right inside the door without a glance and dropped his keys on the small table in the foyer. He stood and looked carefully at himself in the mirror above the table.

Just like this morning when he'd looked in the bathroom mirror, he first noticed the deep lines in the brow. Crow's feet around his eyes and mouth. Brown spots on his forehead. Dark bags under both eyes. Turning 65 was not the pretty picture AARP painted in its publications. Whoever coined the term 'golden years' either had quite the sense of humor or they were blind. Or still young.

He tried smiling, hoping that would improve his appearance. It was a little better, as long as he didn't look too closely at his yellowing teeth. At least they were his own. He still had a full head of snowy hair and bushy white eyebrows that his grandson liked. But he wondered how other people saw him these days.

Inwardly, he fought to hold onto that image of himself from his mid-forties. Strong. Sure. Forthright. That was the figure of Samuel Block he hoped to express. In his prime, he'd been 6'2", though at his last check-up he was down an inch and a half. He straightened up in front of the mirror, trying to pull his shoulders back. He inched upward only to feel a sharp pain between his shoulder blades. His body sank forward to ease the discomfort.

Suddenly, he felt a strong urge to use the bathroom. *Damned prostate.* He'd been on medication for the last four years. It helped, but he still had to go every two to three hours. He hadn't had a full night's sleep in years. Until he was in his late fifties, he never even thought about it, but now he always made sure he included a bathroom break before meetings, dinners, ball games or movies. He hated planning his life around the availability of a toilet. He made a dash for the small half bath in the hallway, quickly turning on the light. The toilet seat was already up.

After washing his hands, he walked into the kitchen which opened up to a modest-sized living room. It was clear he was single. The condo's interior was neat and clean, but it lacked personality. It was utilitarian. A butcher block table and ladder-back chairs. A well-worn couch and an armchair in front of an older TV. No flat screen. His furnishings comprised an accountant's bottom line: simple and in order.

The one slice of his personality on display was a smattering of framed photos on the walls. Most were enlarged photos of Pacific Northwest mountain panoramas. The Olympics, the Cascades, Mount Rainier, Mount St. Helens, Mount Hood. Samuel had been an avid hiker and sought the outdoors whenever he had the time and energy. These photos were his windows to the world he loved.

Samuel took a moment to look more closely at one picture in particular that hung close to the kitchen counter.

It was an 8 x 10 black-and-white photo, somewhat faded since the mid-1960s when it was taken. He and Thad stood on a broad snowfield that stretched to the frosting-like pinnacle of Glacier Peak. They were smiling and making peace signs with both hands. For Samuel, the picture summed up the best parts of his youth.

Samuel turned away from the picture to the blinking light of his answering machine on the counter—and his hopes lifted cautiously with the thought that he might have a congratulatory birthday message or two. He decided to savor the anticipation and get something to eat first.

The contents of his fridge were similar to his furnishings. Simple. He was not a picky person. Though he'd spent a fair amount of time today worrying about his future, he certainly didn't need much to sustain himself in the present. He popped leftover Trader Joe's orange chicken into the microwave and grabbed a key lime yogurt. Reflexively, he checked the expiration date. It had expired last week. He wrinkled his eyes and took a mouthful, thinking about Mel Gibson and Sigourney Weaver in *The Year of Living Dangerously*.

Jeez, what was with him tonight? Old movies and songs. Was he just being nostalgic or was he spending too much time with Netflix? He stared at a second spoonful of lime yogurt for a few moments. He thought to himself, *That which does not kill you....*

When the microwave beeped, he took out the steaming chicken and put it on the table. The tangy smell revived him a bit. Why be depressed? He had a solid roof over his head, plenty of food. And drink! He opened the fridge and grabbed a Black Butte Porter. He might be alone, but he could enjoy a good brew on the brink of his 65th birthday. Not quite champagne, but a good dark beer was a close second. His doctor told him not to drink beer after 5:00, that he'd have to go to the bathroom at least two more times before bed. But what the hell, it was his birthday!

Samuel felt much better after eating. Depositing the paper plate covered in orange goo in the garbage can under the sink, he reached over to his answering machine. He had two messages. He hit the play button with anticipation.

"Grandpa, this is Jimmy. I wanna be first to say happy, happy, happy, happy, happy, happy birthday! Dad says I can't say 'happy' sixty-five times because I'll fill up your machine, but that's what I wanted to do. I'll help you blow out your candles when I see you. Bye, bye. I love you!"

Samuel replayed the message and smiled. His grandson had just delivered a precious gift. Something he needed to hear—that he meant something to someone. *Wasn't that more important than being able to retire to Arizona and play golf?* Of course it was. His son David hadn't reached out to him much since the divorce, but maybe Jimmy would help change that. His grandson's message was better than the icing on any birthday cake.

With a shrill beep that chilled the warmth created by Jimmy's words, the second message automatically began.

"Sam." He heard a voice thick with emotion. "This is Cheri." There was a pause. "There's no good way for you to hear this—or for me to tell you." Her voice cut away, and then came back softly. "Thad died last night. He had a heart attack in his sleep." Stunned, Samuel listened to her recorded sobbing as she whispered, "Call me."

Samuel stared at the answering machine in disbelief. He'd talked to Thad last week. They'd made plans to celebrate his birthday. Thad dead. *How could that be?*

The question was as incomprehensible as the thought of his best friend gone. Taken so quickly. He stared at the photo of Thad and him on the slopes of Glacier Peak.

They'd been inseparable in college, since rooming together as freshmen at the University of Washington. Both had majored in business, thinking that someday they'd be the next Carnegies or Rockefellers. They were always scheming about how they'd make it big in the business world.

But it was really their shared enthusiasm for hiking that made them fast friends. Thad's family had a cabin in the Cascades that had been the starting point for many of their backpacking trips. It was there in the paradise of the mountains crisscrossed by roaring rivers and pearlescent lakes that he and Thad had worn the tread off several pairs of hiking boots. Camping under the Milky Way, inspired by a galaxy so bright with possibilities, they had dreamed and planned their futures.

Then, right out of college, Thad had met Cheri who'd grown up on Bainbridge Island. It didn't take long for Samuel to go from 'best friend' to 'best man.' Thad and Cheri bought a house on Bainbridge and Thad found a job there, while Samuel started working for an accounting firm near Seattle with an eye on opening his own business some day.

Samuel and Thad had stayed close, continuing to camp and hike together—sometimes with their families—almost every summer for 25 years. To Samuel, an only child, Thad was like an older brother. A brother he'd come to depend on in good times—and in bad. He'd always been there. The one person he could always count on. A sounding board. A prankster. A storyteller. A fellow dreamer and adventurer. To Samuel, Thad was family in the truest sense.

Thad gone?

Samuel steadied himself against the counter. He felt weak, his stomach suddenly rolling. *How could life jerk him around like this?* One message from his grandson bringing him warmth and optimism. The next message leaving him numb and nauseous.

With deepening anguish, Samuel lowered himself onto a barstool. For several minutes he sat motionless, frozen by the first icy waves of grief. His mind too full of unanswerable questions, his emotions too raw, any larger message lost.

Finally, he swallowed hard and stood up to make one of the toughest calls of his life. Slowly, Samuel dialed the number that would no longer connect him to his closest friend, only to his newly widowed wife.

THE CROSSING

UNBELIEVABLE, SAMUEL THOUGHT AS HE WAITED
in his car at the ferry terminal. Thad's funeral awaited him.
Four days after Samuel had gotten the news from Cheri.
Three days after he'd turned sixty-five. Twenty-five days
since he received his Medicare Card. Thad had turned
sixty-five three months ago—but he would grow no older.

Samuel had about 20 minutes before the ferry would
arrive and discharge a heavy load of commuters to down-
town Seattle. Sitting in his car and watching the rain
coming down in sheets made his deep sense of sorrow and
loss penetrate further into his being.

He thought about Thad, their time in college, backpacking trips, the weddings of their sons, watching the Mariners,
the Sonics and the Seahawks over beers, and talking shop.
Though Samuel knew he had a tendency towards sarcasm,
Thad just zinged it back at him. Thad could take and dish.
He loved the banter. That made his death even more difficult to accept.

Only days before his heart gave out, they'd spoken on the phone. Casual joking about the hapless state of pro sports teams in Seattle and making plans to toast Samuel's birthday. And just like that, he'd never see Thad again. Never talk to him again. Tears welled up and spilled onto Samuel's cheeks. He had lost his closest, his most dependable, his only real friend. He was alone.

As the mammoth ferry, Klickitat, shuddered heavily into the dock, Samuel's sense of loss stretched out as wide and grey as the leaden skies over Puget Sound. Hundreds of passengers emerged on foot from the upper deck of the ferry and began making their trek over Alaskan Way and then down the stairs onto Western Avenue. At the same time, bicycles, then motorcycles, followed by cars, pickup trucks and several larger commercial trucks emerged from the car deck. As the exodus slowed, people around him started their engines. Samuel stared at the gaping mouth of the vessel as if it were ready to swallow him whole, dragging him down into its vast maw. Never to be seen or heard from again. Just like Thad.

A thousand ways to die. *Which would be his way? What form would his reaper take?* Bleakly, he imagined his death would be slow, tedious and alone. Samuel Block would go out with a whimper, rather than a bang. In the face of his unforgiving mortality, a creeping sense of dread seized him. He gripped the steering wheel desperately as if it was the only thing holding him in this world.

Suddenly, behind him a lone horn honked. Cars in front of him had started moving. Samuel sat still. More horns.

He willed his head to move, to break his frozen stare. He let out a sharp breath and forced his hand to reach down to the ignition, pinch the key and turn it. The car came to life, even if Samuel's mind didn't. He was as numb as the rain that pressed the sky down around him. His car seemed to move forward of its own volition—into the waiting belly of the beast.

The thirty-five minute crossing was a blur of grays: sky and sea inseparable. Samuel had stayed in the Celica, deep in the car deck, hanging on for life. He could've moved to the passenger deck where most drivers fled for the warmth, the cafeteria food and hot drinks, the possibilities for conversation with strangers, or the passing panoramic views of Puget Sound. Today Samuel preferred the isolation of his car, the hypnotic thrumming of the engines, the safety of his cocoon. Just as if he'd been swallowed by his grief.

Losing Thad was like losing a part of himself. He couldn't help but think that this would become a major milestone toward his own end. Thad's death felt in some ways like an accelerant to his own decline.

One by one, acquaintances his age and older would start to pass away. It wasn't like he hadn't experienced death before. Both his parents had died over a decade ago. He'd been to many funerals, but this was a contemporary, his closest friend. Even though he knew Thad had lived a full life, it was over in an instant, and Samuel was brought face to face with his own mortality. How much longer did he really have?

The quality of his own life was slowly sinking. With his medical issues only worsening, his financial future in question, and little chance for new relationships, death looked like a pretty good alternative some days. His best years, his middle years, had come and gone and now he was clearly deteriorating—physically, emotionally and financially.

When Samuel heard the squawking announcement for drivers to return to their cars, he attempted to clear his dark thoughts by counting down—something he'd done since childhood—anticipating when the ferry would make contact with the dock at Bainbridge. He had guessed 30, but was on the number 17 when the ferry gently ricocheted off the huge pilings.

Crew members dressed in slick yellow rain gear tied off the bow. He waited until the cars in front of him began slowly moving forward. He followed closely as he drove up the ramp, feeling a slight sense of relief that he had gotten this far. Yet as he maneuvered his car into the right hand lane, the growing weight of what it would mean to attend the funeral of his best friend of almost 50 years began pressing in on him again. A gradually increasing heaviness, like shovelfuls of dirt being thrown on a coffin.

Samuel clenched the steering wheel to get a better grip, though, deep inside, he felt he was close to losing complete control.

GRIND TIME

SAMUEL DROVE SLOWLY TO THE ISLAND FUNERAL Home. He'd printed out directions from Google Maps but knew it was only one turn off on High School Road. The February day was so dark and heavy, it seemed as if the sun would never shine again. The way he was feeling right now, he wondered if he should be putting down a deposit on his own plot. He sensed he had one toe in the grave anyway.

He didn't know what he'd do when he saw Cheri or Jonathon, their son. Thad had taken so much pride in his son and had spent every moment he could enjoying and developing their relationship as Jonathon grew up. And when Jonathon's son Michael was born, he embraced his grandson with equal fervor. That was one of the reasons he and Thad hadn't hiked as much the last several years. Thad was devoted to his family.

He'd once told Samuel that he didn't buy into the concept of 'quality time.' He'd explained, "I spell *love*, t-i-m-e. It's all about quantity. You gotta make time for the people you care about. Cheri and Jonathon always come first."

Thad had lived by that conviction. He'd coached Jonathon's teams, stayed active in his scouting troop, taught him his love of woodworking—they'd even built a wooden kayak together. Samuel could only imagine the heartbreak and emotional uproar his son would be suffering at his death.

The punishing news of Thad's death had darkened Samuel's already dreary outlook on growing older. He wondered again if death would be a relief. *No more struggles. No more loneliness. No more having to fight the everyday battles of making a living. No more pains, aches, medications. No more feelings. No more.*

He well understood how dangerous these thoughts were. All his life he had battled with mild depression, that spiraling sense of helplessness. He tried to hide it behind sarcasm and biting humor, but sometimes it got the better of him and he slid towards the void of loneliness and self-loathing. But this wasn't the time to give into it. He had to be strong for Cheri and Thad's family. He owed it to Thad, and, on some deeper level, he felt he owed it to himself.

Ten minutes from the ferry dock, he pulled into a parking spot at the funeral home. The lot was nearly full. That didn't surprise Samuel. Thad was an easy guy to like. He was optimistic. His charisma, like a magnet, attracted people. He participated in community events, activities and groups. He made a difference in the many lives he touched.

Samuel opened his car door. The rain, turned mist, had lowered the grey skies. He worried he might just come apart. With no small effort, he climbed out of his Celica. He forced himself to remember one of the long backpacking trips he and Thad had taken in the North Cascades near Canada. There always came that time during each trip when it stopped being fun. No views. No vistas. Crappy weather. Biting bugs. Thad had called it 'grind time.' You just had to put one foot in front of the other. One step at a time. Progress. Get there. Be stronger than your reluctance, your exhaustion. Get over that eternally nagging question: *What am I doing here?*

Samuel knew it was 'grind time' and his feet, at least, responded. One dress shoe in front of the other. He smiled grimly at what Thad might think of his hesitation. He had no doubt Thad would already be inside in the chapel consoling others if Samuel had been the one whose heart had given out first.

As he slowly approached the entrance, he heard the faint strains of organ music. He paused at the front door. Standing at death's doorstep, a tremor, an uncontrollable chill, ran through him. He sensed he was standing at a crossroad in his life. One path led to darkness and despair. The other to light and possibility. Samuel hesitated. He turned back to look at his car. *Escape? Or just another self-made trap?*

Sucking in a deep breath, fighting against rising emotion, his heart pounding in his chest, he opened one of the large oak doors and crossed the threshold, feeling very alone.

JONATHON
AND MICHAEL

A PUNGENT SMELL OF INCENSE AND LILIES GREETED
Samuel as he entered the chapel. He stopped just inside the
door and took in the scene. The chapel was larger than it
looked from the outside and the vaulted ceiling made it
seem even more spacious. The thickset pews formed a "V"
that opened up to a small marble altar upon which rested
a silver urn. Thad.

Or what was left of Thad. Ashes to ashes. Dust to dust.

Samuel steadied himself. He could do this. For Thad.
For Cheri. Suddenly there was Jonathon, Thad's only child,
extending his hand. "Thanks for coming, Uncle Sam."

Samuel almost laughed at the 'Uncle Sam.' It was how
Thad had first introduced him to Jonathon and it had stuck.
They had always teased him about how he'd someday try to
recruit Jonathon for the U.S. Army. But Samuel could not
laugh today, and Jonathon had not said it in teasing, but

with genuine concern and affection. Samuel took his hand, gripped it hard and met the younger man's eyes.

He hadn't seen much of Jonathon in the last few years and the resemblance to his father shocked him a bit. The same high brow, the narrow bridge of the nose and those warm brown eyes. He was seeing Thad standing there in his early forties. Time had turned back to a golden past.

"Jonathon, I can't tell you how sorry I am…" he began. His eyes strayed past Jonathon to the urn, and time came crashing back to the terrible present. His throat tightened, his eyes watered, his grip loosened from Jonathon's. Time stopped.

Jonathon gripped his upper arm in recognition of Samuel's grief and loss. "I know. I can't believe it either. I was just with him last weekend. We met for lunch at the Streamline Diner. Just talking. Had pie for dessert. Just like always." Jonathon's voice cracked. "But there isn't an *always*. There's just *some* time. Sixty-five years is some time. He made that count."

Samuel could only nod. Then there was a small voice at his side.

"Dad, Grandma says she needs you."

Jonathon turned to the boy of nine or ten who'd quietly approached. "Thanks, Michael. Do you remember Mr. Block? Grandpa and I called him Uncle Sam."

"Yes, I remember you, Mr. Block. Grandpa used to tell stories about your hikes." He paused and considered Samuel for a moment before he added, "They were pretty funny stories."

Samuel smiled and noted Thad's brown puppy eyes in his grandson. "Your Grandpa knew how to make me laugh too." Again, Samuel started to choke up and he looked away.

Jonathon squeezed his arm again. "I'll tell Mom you're here. Are you going to be able to make it over to the house after the ceremony?"

"Of course. Of course," Samuel almost whispered.

"I'll let her know. She'll want to see you. I think it'll be easier for her when we're back at the house. See you there."

Jonathon released his grip on Samuel's arm and placed it on Michael's shoulder as they made their way to a side door.

Samuel hadn't been ready for any of this. Thad's death only multiplied his fears about growing older. His own inadequacy. And then, right off the bat, seeing Jonathon—a younger version of Thad. And then his son Michael—an even earlier manifestation of Thad. Samuel couldn't help thinking about his own grandson Jimmy. His heart raced with emotion and he felt unsteady on his feet. His neuroma sent a searing signal through his right foot, so he hurried to the nearest open pew.

He sat down next to a man in a dark pinstriped suit. The fellow, who was clearly older than Samuel, was neat, lean and sat erect in the pew. Samuel, in recent years, had begun to morbidly compare himself to those who seemed older. It was as if he could make himself feel younger by trying to imagine how those around him were breaking down faster than he was. He guessed the man to be ten to fifteen years his senior. Somehow that made him feel better—like there were other folks at the front of the line when the grim reaper came knocking.

It was a horrible thought. Made more horrible when the man smiled kindly at him and nodded. How could Samuel be so low, so self-centered? Death had claimed his best friend, someone who deserved to be alive—much more so than Samuel with his petty thoughts. In reply to the older man's nod, he hung his head, hiding his shame under the veil of grief.

A Not-About-You Eulogy

SAMUEL HELD HIS DOWNWARD GAZE, LIFTING it only when the organ music changed pace. A priest in simple vestments emerged from the side door in the chapel, followed by Cheri, then a woman whom Samuel did not recognize immediately, followed by Jonathon and his wife Marie, and their children, Michael and Lauren.

The priest led them to the front row. He stepped onto the altar and turned to face the chapel full of mourners as the family members solemnly seated themselves. Cheri and the woman sat, side-by-side, hands clasped. Then it clicked. She was Thad's sister, Sarah.

Samuel had met her a few times when he and Thad had been in college. Sarah was a few years younger, so she hadn't really registered as socially compelling to Samuel. Thad would sometimes bring up something about her or she'd show up in one of his family stories about growing up with a sister—either they'd be fighting over the phone, what TV programs to watch or who should get to use the bathroom first in the morning (because Sarah took *forever* to get ready). Though, Thad also shared childhood stories of them hiking near their family's cabin on the Salmon la Sac River in the North Cascades. As kids, they'd pack a lunch and take off to hike and explore and be gone the entire day. They might've competed at home for the phone, TV, and bathroom, but they had both inherited a love of the outdoors.

Samuel recalled that Sarah had gone to college on the East Coast and eventually married and settled in Virginia. If he was remembering correctly, her husband had worked for some government agency in DC. He really hadn't heard too much from Thad about her over the years, although he did know her first marriage had gone sour rather quickly. He'd last seen her at Jonathon's wedding, but they hadn't spoken. Samuel had heard from Thad that Sarah had recently moved to Port Townsend, just an hour or so north on Puget Sound. Thad liked having her back in the area and Sarah was equally happy being closer to family.

How hard it must be for her, he thought. *To lose your only brother.* He focused on Cheri and Sarah and wondered what could be going through their minds. They both sat very still, their eyes fixed on the priest.

When the organ music ended, the chapel became stony quiet. The priest took a deep breath, and then introduced himself as Father Langston. He lifted his arms in greeting and thanked everyone for coming. All through the next part of the service, Samuel heard the words being spoken, but they didn't really register. It was as if he was watching himself listen to the kind words being said about a man named Thaddeus Brian Curtis. Father Langston began by reading two psalms which he related to Thad's qualities of generosity and compassion. When he finished, Jonathon rose and told several heartfelt stories that emphasized Thad's commitment as a husband, father and grandfather.

It should have been moving for Samuel, but the praise and admiration for his friend—his best and only true friend—fell flat. Terrible emotions clawed at him. On one level, the praise depressed him. Thad had seemed to be everything he wanted to be. Samuel's own life felt empty and without purpose by comparison. On another level, the accolades angered him. *Why was Thad gone? He was so loved, so respected. He deserved to be alive.* Thad had so much more to live for, much more to give to those around him. Much more than Samuel felt he had at that moment.

His bout of bitterness and self-pity was, mercifully, interrupted when Jonathon finished speaking and the older man next to him quietly said, "Excuse me. Can I get by?"

Samuel reflexively swung his legs to the side and watched as the older man made his way up the aisle and stepped behind the podium. Samuel was surprised into attentiveness. *Who was this? Why was he speaking about Thad?*

The older man began. His eyes were clear. His voice had a steady and strong rhythm. "For those who don't know me, let me introduce myself. My name is Ben Broader. I haven't known Thad as long as most of you, but Cheri asked me to speak because she felt that Thad's involvement in our Eldering Circle over the past three years made an important difference in his life. Honestly, it was the other way around. Thad made a difference in the lives of everyone around him. That is what Eldering is about. Leveraging the wisdom and experience of a lifetime to help others.

"When Thad first became involved in our group, he was restless. He was searching for something, and he didn't know what that 'something' was. Most people tend to think that impatience happens only to the young or to mid-life males who impulsively buy red convertibles in answer to the question 'Is this all there is?' But that's not always the case. Thad was a perfect example. He felt that there was more for him to do, more to live for. He didn't need some 'thing.' He needed something more."

Samuel was bewildered. From his perspective, Thad had it all. A great wife and family, financial security, and seemingly good health. *What was this Ben Broader fellow talking about?*

"Through our Eldering meetings, Thad's view of life, who he was, and what he could contribute, grew. He became involved in several community programs, mentoring at-risk teens, delivering for Meals on Wheels. He joined in with the local Scout troop, lending his carpentry skills when they did some much needed maintenance on Fran Wilker's house. She told me later that Thad had returned the week after to install more insulation around the outside doors. Thad was also considering running for the school board—at the age of 65! Thad had truly come to understand what Eldering is all about. It is the recognition of life's total journey and that each stage of the journey requires determination, sacrifice and purpose. I only wish Thad's journey could've lasted longer. I thank you, Cheri, for letting me express what Thad has meant to our Eldering Circle and our community."

Ben's clear eyes misted up as he finished. Before he could leave the podium, Father Langston joined him and put his hand on Ben's shoulder. "Like Ben, I belong to the Eldering Circle. And as he said, there is growth in every stage of life—from childhood and adolescence through adulthood, middle age and old age. Thad discovered that, at each stage, you have to let go of some things to move forward. Like all of us entering into that later stage of our lives, Thad had to let go of any resentment or bitterness about growing older in order to move forward and reclaim his sense of purpose and his passion for what could still be accomplished with the rest of his life.

"Thad wasn't what you would call a devout Christian, but I witnessed in him a very spiritual side—for he seemed to implicitly understand what Jesus meant in Matthew 16:25 when he said 'For anyone who wants to save his life will lose it, but anyone who loses his life for my sake will find it.' Thad came to see that there is a tremendous spirituality to aging that can turn losses into gains, weaknesses into strengths. He came to see that letting go of fear can lead to a new life: a life lived for others. A life committed to sharing the best of who he was in a way that brought out

29

the best in those around him. Let us remember him in that way—*always.*"

The priest crossed himself. Ben returned and sat down next to Samuel. The organist played a final hymn. The service was almost at an end. Yet Samuel, far from being comforted and calmed, was rolling over a very petty and vexing question. *Why had his best friend never spoken to him about Ben Broader and this Eldering group?*

SENSE AND SENSIBILITY

AFTER THE SERVICE SAMUEL WAS TOO DISMAYED with himself to stay in the chapel and mingle. His mood matched the heavy February rain that continued to pour down as he sat in his car, trying to understand what had just happened. Why was he so filled with bitterness and accusation? Was this normal grief? Or was he being small and trivial? Was he envious of the outpouring of love for Thad? Was he jealous of Ben Broader's personal connection to Thad which seemed, after only a few years, to be more important than all the years he'd called Thad his best friend? Or was he hurt that Thad seemed to have found an answer to all the physical and emotional turmoil Samuel was now dealing with as he aged—and not shared it with him?

The questions nagged at him. He couldn't go to Cheri's house in this state of mind. *What good would that do?* He had almost resolved to return to the ferry dock and cross back to Seattle when he saw through his rain-streaked windshield Jonathon escorting Cheri to their car. Michael was holding an umbrella to shield his grandmother from the downpour. A simple act of kindness, of caring, of love.

Samuel was confronted with the sense and sensibility of Michael's act. It reminded him of his own grandson, Jimmy. It wasn't that complicated. *Protect the ones you love. Care for them. Nurture them. Simply and unconditionally.* Samuel understood this credo, but lately he'd become too focused on his own problems. He had allowed himself to become pathetic. Insignificant. Afraid.

Ben Broader and Father Langston had said a mouthful when they'd said Thad knew how to live for others. Samuel didn't know how to do that. And he sensed that perhaps that was what was at the heart of his own problems.

As he watched Cheri being helped into the car by Michael, he inwardly recognized that Thad—his most trusted friend—was pointing him towards another journey. Not a grueling fifty-mile hike seesawing along the Pacific Crest Trail. Samuel was going it solo now on a much tougher trail—a painful path of truth and self-discovery.

As he started his car, preparing to follow Jonathon and Cheri, he wondered whether he could lift himself above the drabness of the weather and the despair in his own heart. Was he ready for the journey which the spirit of his trekking buddy seemed to be coaxing him?

A Broader Sense

IT WASN'T EASY. MORE OF THAT 'GRIND TIME' that only Thad could smile at during the most tedious and arduous parts of their hikes together. But Samuel had not only made it to the house, he'd made it inside. He'd talked with Jonathon again and then made small talk with a few folks he'd come in contact with over the years through Thad.

He still hadn't approached Cheri. She and Sarah, who'd remained close by her side since the funeral, had been surrounded by a host of friends extending their condolences since he'd arrived. He knew he would eventually have to speak to Thad's widow, but as time passed, he felt it was going to be harder and harder to do.

He made his way to the dining room where a bounty of food occupied one end of the long dining room table to the other. He was looking for a plate, but before he could locate one someone behind him said, "They're over here."

He turned and saw a sideboard stacked with plates, silverware and napkins. The older man who'd spoken at Thad's funeral was holding out a plate to Samuel—who hesitated, a feeling of resentment rising in him.

The old man nodded kindly. Samuel clenched his jaw as if to suppress the inexplicable hostility that arose in him. Samuel knew his feelings were totally irrational, but still he had to forcefully command his hand forward, inch by inch, to accept the plate.

"Thanks," Samuel said when he finally took hold of it.

"No problem. My name's Ben Broader. We sat next to each other during the funeral, remember?"

"Yes. I remember," Samuel said tautly, and then forced himself to go on. "You spoke about Thad. It was … it was…."

Samuel had to turn away. When he faced the older man again, Ben was looking at him sympathetically. "Funerals are never easy—for lots of reasons. And most of them don't have anything to do with death. Why don't you get some food and perhaps we can talk later."

As the old man turned to go, Samuel was struck by how quickly Ben had assessed the situation, sensed the struggle he was going through and given him the space he was craving. In a rush of mixed emotions, Samuel spluttered, "Sorry, uh, Ben. Didn't mean to be rude. Just not myself today."

"It's okay. It's a tough day for all of us."

"Let me just grab something to eat, then I'd like to ask you about what you said at the service."

"Certainly, Samuel," Ben said with an easy smile.

Samuel's eyes widened. "How'd you know my name?"

Ben Broader's smile widened in return. "Thad was very fond of telling stories of his wilderness escapades, and I've seen quite a few photos of you two on mountain tops. I know you've been great friends since college. I envy you that."

Envy? Wasn't that what he'd been feeling during Ben's eulogy? He took a small step back from Ben and suddenly a searing bolt shot up through his right foot and went straight to his brain. He winced hard at the neuroma-induced pain.

"You okay, Samuel?"

After a long sucking breath, Samuel replied, "Yeah. I just need to get off my feet."

"Why don't you go find yourself a chair and I'll grab you some food. What would you like?"

As he hobbled back towards the living room, Samuel called back, "Surprise me." Because Ben Broader already had.

FIRST STEPS

IRONICALLY, SAMUEL'S FIRST STEP TOWARDS letting go of his bitterness at Thad's death and his own fears about growing older meant getting off his feet. He sat down on the bench of the upright piano and was struck by a memory of Thad tinkling out "Happy Birthday" when Jonathon was a small boy. Cheri was the musician in their family, but Thad would try anything—especially if it put a smile on someone's face. Sitting on the smooth, well-worn wood of the familiar bench, Samuel immediately felt better. Both the pain in his foot and the ache in his heart eased somewhat.

Ben Broader arrived a few moments later with a plate of food and a bottle of Anchor Steam beer. It had always been one of Thad's personal favorites. He handed Samuel the bottle. "I thought if the food selection didn't surprise you, this might."

In spite of himself, Samuel smiled. "Thanks. This'll be great." He accepted the beer with his right hand and then balanced the plate of food on his lap with his left. "Are you going to get something?"

"I snacked a little when I first got here, so I'm good." Ben nodded towards Samuel's bottle of beer. "I might join you a bit later with a drink, but I don't want to have to be running off to the bathroom during our talk."

"Let me guess. Prostate problems?" Samuel commiserated. "Drives me nuts."

"Well, you get old enough, every guy has prostate problems. My doc told me once that if a man is lucky enough to reach a 100, he only has two things to worry about: prostate cancer or being hit by a bus."

Samuel chuckled and raised his beer. "I'll drink to that."

Ben nodded. "I wish I could blame it all on my prostate. An old Navy buddy of mine used to say to me, 'Broader, you never *buy* beer—you only *rent* it!'"

Again, Samuel laughed. He was beginning to see why Thad might've liked and trusted this guy. "Do you want to pull up a chair?" Samuel asked.

"That I do." He ducked around to the dining room and quickly returned with a folding chair. He placed it to Samuel's side and sat down. "That's better. Always good to take a load off."

"Yeah," Samuel agreed, stretching out his right foot. "Especially when the neuroma is acting up. Getting old can really be a pain." He smiled grimly, intending it as an invitation for Ben to share his own complaints about aging. Surely, Samuel thought, Ben would have a lot to complain about.

37

But Ben didn't bite. He looked directly and seriously at Samuel. "Is that the way it feels to you? That getting old is about breaking down—a slow, aching descent to death?"

Samuel was surprised by Ben's earnestness, the sheer concern of his question. "Well, look around the room. We're not exactly here to celebrate our youth. Thad's dead because his body gave out. It betrayed him. It's what we all face."

Ben didn't respond immediately. When he did, he was apologetic. "Sorry. I kind of went 'psychotherapist' on you. I didn't intend to. Lots of people confuse health with well-being. I just have different ideas about what growing older means. What it can mean."

"Like what you said during the eulogy?"

"Exactly. Getting old doesn't have to be full of regret or bitterness. The physical challenges are always there, but it's one's spirit, one's sense of purpose that counts. If your personal drive deserts you, that's really the death knell. Luckily for Thad, when he heard the bell, he didn't wait around and listen to it count down. He heeded the call and took action."

"You mean Thad knew he was going to die soon?"

"No. It wasn't like he had a premonition of the heart attack that took his life. Thad was, like all of us, growing older, asking a lot of questions we put off when we're in the thick of starting a career or raising a family or maintaining a lifestyle. I'm sure you've experienced that, Samuel."

Samuel nodded in response. It seemed that was exactly what occupied a lot of his free time: mentally replaying uncomfortable questions about his future.

Ben continued. "Thad felt his sense of usefulness and purpose drifting and he got involved in our Eldering Circle. He wanted to become an Elder."

"I guess that's what I really wanted to ask you about. You mentioned that when you spoke and I had no idea what it was," Samuel admitted. He paused, not sure how to conceal the stab of hurt he'd felt that Thad had never told him about this group.

"Thad never told me about it. I just wondered why. Is it like the Masons? Secret handshakes and all that?"

Ben smiled. "I wish we were that organized. Eldering is not some kind of secret society. It's more a viewpoint, a way of approaching life—especially the last decades of our lives."

Samuel took a sip of his beer without losing eye contact with Ben.

"As I grew to know Thad, I realized something about him. He preferred to lead by example. He wanted what Eldering taught him to shine through in how he began to live his life. He felt that taking positive action would get others thinking, 'Wow. I want to be involved like that guy.'"

"Yeah, Thad was the kind of person who had to fully understand something before he'd share it. He disliked half answers," Samuel asserted.

"And I'm betting Thad hadn't told you because he was waiting to become an Elder. He was waiting, possibly, so he could mentor you."

"Mentor me?"

"That's one of the responsibilities after becoming an Elder. Mentoring to develop other Elders. We're a movement. Boomers and beyond. So I'm sure Thad planned to invite you to his Eldering Ceremony—and then cajole you to follow him on this journey of ours to revitalize our community and our nation. To give back to our world."

"An Eldering Ceremony?" Samuel asked in surprise. "So this is a formal thing? Are people recruited to 'revitalize our nation' or something? Do you have to apply and be accepted? How does this work and how did Thad get involved?"

"It's not at all mysterious or hard to get involved in Eldering. The first step is learning about it. The second is wanting to get involved," Ben explained. "I think you've just taken the first step."

Ben stopped talking suddenly and quietly stood up. He was staring past Samuel. Samuel turned. He quickly set his food to the side and stood as well.

Thad's sister, Sarah, was standing there. Her eyes reddened, but bright. Her hand gently held out in greeting.

SARAH

BEN WAS THE FIRST TO TAKE HER HAND. "I'M SO sorry for your loss," he said.

"I wanted to thank you for your kind words about Thad. I know you did a lot for him, Mr. Broader."

"His example is one that needs to be shared. I truly admired your brother."

Sarah's cheeks reddened, but she did not cry. "So did I. He accomplished so much. He really knew how to live." She held out her hand to Samuel. "Which I'm sure 'Uncle Sam' here can attest to."

They shook hands warmly. "Yes, he did know how to live. No one had to teach him that," Samuel said and released her hand. "It's been a long time, Sarah. I'm…I'm very sorry."

She nodded politely, as if she hadn't heard those same words a thousand times in the last week. "I want to talk to both of you, but first Cheri also wants me to convey her greetings. She's been smothered since she got home and she wants to speak with you both later. She's hoping you'll be able to stay until things settle down and she has the chance to see you."

"Of course," said Samuel. Ben nodded his intent as well.

Sarah looked down at Samuel's plate of food. "That looks good. I think I'll go get something myself. Do you mind if I join you?"

"Would you like me to get you something?" Ben offered.

Sarah hesitated and then said, "Thank you, yes."

"Here, take my chair and I'll be right back. Anything in particular?"

"Oh," she said sitting down exhaustedly in the chair, "Surprise me."

"Boy, you two really trust me," Ben said with an expression of mock alarm.

Not knowing exactly what Ben was referring to, Sarah said, "Thad certainly trusted you, so I'm on board."

Ben slipped around to the dining room, and Samuel sat back down on the piano bench. "How are you holding up?" he asked.

"It comes in waves, as you probably know. I seem to do better around others, but when I'm on my own, it'll just sneak up on me. Thad is gone. No more of his laughter, his practical jokes, his confidence, his voice. No matter what, Thad and I could always talk." Her voice dropped to a wistful half whisper. "But most of all, he was my big brother. My protector."

She dabbed at the corners of her eyes with a tattered wad of tissue she held in her left hand. "Sorry. Oh, boy. Enough crying already!"

Samuel nodded in understanding.

She paused and took a slow, deep breath. "So, how are you, Sam? I can't think of how long it's been."

"I was thinking about that when I saw you in the chapel. I remember you being at Jonathon's wedding, but I don't think we've talked since before you got married."

"Four decades." Sarah looked slowly around the room. "Hard to believe time can move that fast. And look at me. Two marriages, actually. No children. Several different jobs. Now, Thad's death. What about you?"

Samuel wasn't all that surprised at Sarah's bluntness. She'd always been a pistol, ready to say what was on her mind, trying to one up Thad if he teased her. She'd said Thad was her protector, but Samuel knew she could take care of herself. And she had. In spite of her red eyes, she looked strong. Her complexion was clear, her features still firm. Though tired, she still exuded a vibrancy and charisma.

"Well," he began, "I'm still an accountant, the only thing I've ever done. My marriage fell apart thirteen years ago. My son David is married and I have a grandson, Jimmy, who's six. I don't see them as much as I'd like. Plus, I've got a medicine cabinet stocked to the gills. You know, a little help from my doctor friends to get me by."

Sarah gave a smile of recognition. "I guess we're living the dream, eh?" She said it lightly, but both of them seemed to sense an underlying gravity. The mood became pensive.

Ben intervened in their awkward silence by reappearing with a plateful of food in a much more decorous arrangement for Sarah. "I hope this will do. Would you like something to drink as well? Water? Wine?"

"Thank you, Ben. This is lovely." She glanced over at the Anchor Steam sitting on the piano bench by Samuel. "I do like my wine, but if it's not too much trouble, I'll have what Samuel's drinking. Thad used to encourage me to expand my palate. He'd be proud to see me try one of the microbrews he loved so much."

"One of his best qualities," Samuel cut in, slightly tipping the top of his bottle.

"Sounds like a good idea. I may just have to join you," Ben said as he departed again to get two beers.

"He certainly is a nice man," Sarah commented. "I wasn't sure what to make of this Eldering thing Thad had become involved in. In fact, I'm not sure Thad ever mentioned that all his volunteering had anything to do with Ben or a specific organization. But you know Thad. He was all about doing, not self-promoting."

"That's for sure. I'd never heard about Ben or Eldering from Thad either." Samuel was oddly reassured by the fact that Sarah seemed to be in the dark as well.

Ben returned with two open bottles and handed one to Sarah along with a fresh napkin. "Here you go."

Samuel scooted over on the piano bench. "Sit down, Ben."

"Thanks," Ben said as he took a seat. "Were you able to catch up a bit?"

"Yes," Sarah answered. "It's been a while. We haven't seen much of each other since our early twenties. It's like blinking. And now we're in our sixties. Kind of a weird experience. To go from being young to being old, just like that."

Ben chuckled. "I wouldn't say you're old. I'm 84, and I just consider myself *vintage*."

"*Vintage*. That's an appealing way to look at it," Sarah said. "Is that how you got Thad interested in Eldering?"

"Well, I was explaining that to Samuel a little earlier. Eldering is a way to view your life experience. *Vintage* might not really be the right term. Folks tend to think of 'classic cars' and 'well-maintained' whenever I say it. You also hear the clichés, you know, that we're becoming 'fine wine' or 'aging gracefully.' Personally, I want to add 'sepia studs' to that list."

"*Sepia studs*. I kind of like that," Samuel interjected. "Though I think I'd need to Photoshop a lot of my old pictures first."

"Wouldn't we all," Ben rejoined. "I guess my point is that an older person is not an automobile or a bottle of wine. Those kinds of metaphors can create comparisons that are too simplistic. People are complicated. And aging is complex. But it stands to reason that the longer you're on this planet, the more you know about how things work and what's important. You should be accruing capital that creates wisdom."

"That kind of makes sense, but understanding how things work and being wise, aren't those two different things?" Samuel asked.

"For me, being wise is about sharing the best of who I am—my perspective, my experience, my way of being in the world—with others in a way that brings out the best in them."

Samuel's eyes narrowed skeptically. "How do you do that?"

"Well, I talk with people about being informed and committed enough to manage a healthy lifestyle, a lifestyle that matches their interests and purpose. This 'wisdom' comes from my personal experience—from my understanding of how life works as a human being, with needs and hopes and a desire to belong and make a difference. We all need to have a purpose and Eldering is a way of living the rest of your life with a sense of purpose," Ben explained.

"Was Thad really feeling that directionless when he came to you?" Sarah asked.

"He didn't come to me," Ben admitted. "He'd participated in several retreats with Father Langston and spoken with him. I've known Jack—Father Langston—for most of my adult life. We began the Eldering Circle here on Bainbridge. So Jack invited Thad to one of our meetings."

"So it's affiliated with the church, then?" Samuel asked, trying to get a bead on Eldering.

"No. Eldering is about finding purpose through giving back to others. In that sense, it can be spiritually uplifting. But we don't preach a particular creed, if that's what you're asking."

"So, is it more like a support group where you meet regularly to talk about what's going on in your life?" Sarah asked.

"Boy, you two may have more questions than Carter's got pills."

Sarah and Samuel looked at each other, then back at Ben.

"Carter's liver pills." Ben chuckled. "Just an old expression. I don't mind dating myself. And I really don't mind your questions.

"In an Eldering Circle, we support each other in becoming and being Elders. We discuss where we see opportunities for giving back to the community, for sharing the best of who we are every day. We are trying to shift the general attitude about aging. That's what really inspired Thad: the possibility of continuing to make a difference every day for the rest of his life."

Ben paused. "I can go on and on, but I'm not here to sell you on Eldering. I just wanted to explain why people like Thad get involved."

Sarah raised her hand to stifle a yawn, more out of fatigue than waning interest. "And I do appreciate that, Ben," Sarah said. "I'd like to hear more, but this fine food and beer are starting to fog my brain. I think I'm going to step outside for a little fresh air."

Samuel surprised himself by rising and saying, "Mind if I join you? I could use a little island air myself—even if it's only 50 degrees."

Sarah smiled and replied, "I'd like the company. Ben, you want to join us?"

"I appreciate the offer," he replied, "but I'm going to mingle some more. I'll catch up with you two later."

Tentatively, Samuel extended his hand to Sarah.

FRESH AIR

SARAH TOOK SAMUEL'S HAND AND ROSE FROM
her chair. They dropped off their dishes in the kitchen and
stepped onto the back deck that tiered gracefully down to
the lawn which was bordered by a stand of grand Madrona
and Douglas fir trees beyond. Those trees were Thad's
pride and joy. The house was lovely, but it was the trees
with the backdrop of towering Olympic Mountains that
had sold him on the property. Stepping onto the deck was
like standing at the trailhead of a hike.

Samuel thought about his last major backpacking trip
with Thad. It was almost ten years ago: a trip to celebrate
their 55th birthdays. Toleak Point. A rugged three-day
outing along the northern Washington coast through rain-
forest with some serious scrambling up and down the steep
banks along that wind-carved and isolated stretch. Samuel
had almost backed out because of the timing. It was right
after tax season and he was seriously out of shape. "No
pain, no gain," Thad had chided him.

He'd been right, of course. The hike had been outstanding and Samuel had thoroughly enjoyed himself—even with the steep climbs. Standing on Thad's back deck now, he knew how right his friend had been to get him to push himself and go to Toleak. *No pain, no gain.*

He looked over at Sarah who, too, seemed lost in a private daydream. "Brings back a lot of memories, doesn't it?"

Sarah nodded. "I was just thinking about the birthday party we had for Jonathon last summer. He was downplaying it because he was turning 39 and Thad was ribbing him that soon he wouldn't be such a 'kid' anymore. So he told everyone who was coming to bring a gift that a ten-year-old would enjoy." Sarah grinned at the memory, and then continued with a smile in her eyes.

"You should've seen it. Jonathon got G.I. Joes, Ninja swords, and the board game, *Operation.* He was howling with every gift he opened, but I think Michael and Lauren were thinking this was the best grown-up birthday party they'd ever been to.

"After Jonathon had finished opening presents, Thad brought out two boxes he'd hidden on the side of the deck. A big one and a smaller one. He gave Jonathon the smaller box. Suspiciously, Jonathon opened it and pulled out a super soaker. It was full.

"All of a sudden, Thad yells, 'It's on!' and opened the larger box and started handing out full super soakers to the rest of us. It finally dawned on Jonathon what Thad had in store and he took off running." Sarah began laughing and pointing to the trees beyond the lawn. "Jonathon was soaked before he could take cover. It was an epic water fight. Thad was so good at that. Creating memories."

Samuel nodded. "Yeah. He seemed to have it all figured out—which makes this even tougher." A wave of inadequacy washed over Samuel. The feeling that he could never measure up to Thad, his enthusiasm for people, for life. *What kind of legacy, what kind of stories will I leave behind? What do I have to offer anyone?* he wondered.

"He and Cheri always seemed so perfect," Sarah continued. "I marveled at how they managed to stick together and actually become closer; that's not how it turned out in either of my marriages. I pretty much blamed it on my former spouses, until I realized that it probably had more to do with my own lousy choices. Such is life."

Samuel thought about what Sarah was saying. "I guess when you really delve deeply into any failed relationship there's always enough blame to go around," he admitted. "I blamed Dorothy when we split up because she walked out on me, but living alone for more than a dozen years has given me some perspective. I can be a workaholic who worries a lot about things. I can get pessimistic. I guess that's why I gravitated towards optimists like Dorothy and Thad. Thad probably would have walked out on our friendship a long time ago if he'd had to put up with me 24/7."

Samuel was surprised when Sarah gently put her arm on his. "You're one of Thad's oldest friends. He thought of you as a brother."

"Maybe a cranky one."

"Well, then I must have been his cranky sister. Believe me, with two divorces I've had my share of therapy."

"Really? Did it help?" Samuel asked. He'd never considered therapy even in the darkest times following his divorce.

"Some. It didn't really matter how a therapist labeled my issues. What helped the most was having a good listener. Like you."

Samuel stepped back in surprise, "Me? Oh boy, that's not what Dorothy used to say."

"Well, it's a good thing we're all entitled to our own opinions." A breeze kicked up and Sarah shivered. "I think I'm ready to go back inside."

"Sounds good," Samuel agreed. He placed his hand lightly on her elbow, gesturing her toward the door. His hand on her arm, Samuel felt goose bumps and knew it was not entirely from the cool, reviving air.

A Hill of Beans

THE REST OF THE AFTERNOON PASSED SLOWLY for Samuel. Sarah had gone back to check on Cheri, and he'd found himself pressed into small talk with neighbors and former business associates. At one point, his neuroma began to hurt him so badly he took refuge in the family room on the couch watching Michael, Lauren and other kids playing video games.

He actually dozed off and was nudged awake by Ben. "Sorry to wake you, Samuel. Cheri is exhausted and needs to take a nap. A lot of folks are leaving, but she was hoping you'd be able to stick around until six or so. She wants to meet with the immediate family and some close friends."

Samuel checked his watch. It was about 4:30. He knew the latest ferry back to Seattle was at 11:00, so that wouldn't be a problem. He just wondered what he'd do for the next hour and a half.

"I was thinking about going to grab a coffee. There's a great shop in town, if you'd like to come along," Ben offered, as if reading Samuel's mind.

Samuel rubbed his eyes and tried to shake the cobwebs loose. "Sure," he replied, distracted again by his growing concern over what he'd say to Cheri later that evening.

Ben drove a Toyota Prius. Somehow Samuel had pictured him driving a Buick or a Lincoln, like a lot of people his age. A Prius just didn't fit his expectation of Ben. It was probably the same kind of disconnect younger drivers experienced when they saw him driving his Celica. It wasn't exactly a 65-year-old's typical ride. As for the Prius, Samuel had seen hundreds of the hybrids on the road, but he'd never ridden in one. The car was spooky quiet.

"Does it take a while to get used to this? I kind of like to hear the engine running."

"You get used to it pretty quickly," Ben explained. "You just have to be careful about sneaking up on cyclists and pedestrians. They often don't hear the car coming. Other than that, it's been great. I still do a lot of traveling, and I kind of feel like it's my way of making up for all the CO_2 I've pumped into our atmosphere over decades of driving."

"Never too late to go green, I guess," Samuel said.

"*Never too late* is a great way to operate as you age," Ben said as the Prius glided into a small strip mall. "Here we are."

As Ben pulled into a parking space, Samuel looked up at the shop's sign. The top half was a painting of a squinting Humphrey Bogart with his trademark hat and trench coat hunched over a steaming mug of coffee. Underneath was the name of the shop: *A Hill of Beans.*

"Clever," Samuel said, acknowledging the reference to

the movie *Casablanca*. "I didn't know Bainbridge Island had become so existential."

"This place is more for hedonists. Especially if you get one of the macaroons to go with your coffee," Ben offered with a smile.

In the shop Samuel followed Ben's suggestion and ordered a macaroon. "Thanks for the tip, Ben," he commented after his first bite. "This is excellent. More evidence that old dogs like us can learn new tricks."

"One would hope."

"Is that what the Eldering process is about? Old dogs, new tricks?"

"I think if Eldering had a slogan it would be something like *make the rest of your life be the best of your life*," Ben said.

"Catchy," Samuel said, "But what if your life so far hasn't felt fulfilling or satisfying?" His tone challenged. "Mine is just a grind to make ends meet. How's it supposed to get better?"

"Life is always about the challenge to discover one's potential," Ben began, unfazed. "Not just when you're young. I personally hate to see older folks give up that challenge. Too often, around sixty or sixty-five, most of us cross a preconceived line and begin to see the rest of our lives as a downhill slide."

"Bingo!" Samuel barked, mocking his own viewpoint on growing old as well as the often stereotyped senior pastime.

Well, try this," Ben suggested. "Imagine it's twenty years from now and you're reading your obituary. What would it say? Think about it. Is it how you want to be remembered? Is it how you want to live your life now? Do you think it's too late to make a change?"

Samuel's eyes glazed as he envisioned the sparse obituary marking his death in the paper. "I think I see what you're getting at," he conceded.

"Eldering is just one way of thinking about who we are, about our future, about creating a way of living appropriate to our age and circumstances that allows us to remain positive, vital and engaged. I never want to see people give up—to surrender, to kneel in defeat and to give in to death." Ben's voiced trailed off. "I saw too much of that during the war."

"World War II?" Samuel asked, somewhat in awe.

"Enlisted in the Navy in '42 when I was sixteen. I'd grown up in Iowa and thought I'd change the world, but it worked the other way around. The world, the war, changed me. I was a midshipman aboard the USS Harder, part of a submarine fleet on the offensive against Japan. Ours was the only sub that survived our mission. Thousands of men lost their lives on both sides. It gnawed at me that I couldn't stop it, and that I was actively contributing to the death of so many."

"What did you do after the war?" Samuel wanted to know how Ben had dealt with that burden.

"Same as most soldiers. Tried to forget. Move on. Live the American Dream. And I guess I did. I went to the University of Washington on the GI Bill and earned a business degree. I met my wife Darlene there. We had two children, who are now living in California and Arizona along with my three grandchildren." Ben pointed out the window at the grey, socked-in sky. "They're more sun worshippers than I am.

"I had a solid business consulting firm until I retired in '97. Darlene and I became snowbirds, visiting the kids in the winter months and spending our summers up here. Then Darlene died in 2000. We had over fifty beautiful years together. That, in a nutshell, is Ben Broader's life and it's been a good one. But the whole point is that I'm not done yet. I'm not satisfied."

"Don't you feel like you deserve a break? Some kind of rest?" Samuel probed.

"From what? From trying to help others? From interacting with other people? Making friends? That's not how I see it. Who needs a break from living a fulfilling life?"

"I don't know, Ben." Samuel looked straight into Ben's eyes, searching for something before he decided to go on. "For me, it's just such an effort to keep my head above water. My accounting business is stagnant in this slow economy. My health keeps fighting me. I'm on several medications that take a chunk out of my paycheck and my psyche. And I only expect it to get worse. That's why I'm not looking forward to getting older. You seem to have found some kind of secret. You're pretty quick-witted and spry for 84 and you're positive about your future. Boy, if that's what you and this Eldering can do, then maybe I should sign up."

Ben slowly shook his head. "Believe me, Samuel, when I tell you that the change you're looking for won't come from me or from Eldering. It's going to have to come from *you*."

CHERI'S PLAN

THEY STAYED AT THE COFFEE HOUSE UNTIL almost six o'clock. Ben explained to Samuel that change was all about personal commitment. He used the example of his own personal pledge to stay fit, telling Samuel how he watched his diet, worked out daily at Island Fitness and stayed active with the Eldering Circle.

"It takes motivation and work," Ben explained. "You've got to nurture both the health of the body and the well-being of the spirit. A lot of folks get overly focused on the physical aspect and don't understand the importance of finding fulfillment. Well-being is about achieving that balance of health and purpose.

"My personal goal is to give as much back to my community as I can. It motivates me to stay active and take risks. That was something Thad intrinsically understood. You have to give in order to grow. He saw that clearly and embraced it."

At that point in the conversation, they had to leave and

drive back to the house. On the way, Ben turned his attention to Samuel's life, asking about his family. Samuel told him about his divorce, and the distance he felt from his son and his grandson.

Ben noted to Samuel how his tone lit up when talking about his grandson. "It's so easy to see how much you care about Jimmy. That's the key, Samuel," he explained. "Finding what really matters and making that the focus of your life. That's where the path to becoming an Elder starts: discovering the passion and purpose that energizes you."

By the time they were pulling up at Cheri's, Samuel felt like he'd gotten the message. Eldering was not some silver bullet that would keep the demons of aging at bay. Samuel would have to commit to some serious changes in his outlook and lifestyle if he wanted what it could offer. But he kept coming up with reasons why it wouldn't work for him. He sensed that might be his biggest hurdle.

It was only when he stepped out of Ben's car that he realized he had an even bigger hurdle to top momentarily. When he walked through the door, he'd be face-to-face with Cheri. Thad was his best friend, but he was Cheri's life partner. Her soul mate. What could he possible say to lessen her loss?

He tried to clear his head. He stood poised at the front door while Ben knocked. Jonathon opened the door. "Come in, come in. Thanks for coming back," he said as he ushered them in. "We're gathering in the kitchen. Mom says that's where you should always do your family business—because you're never too far from the chocolate."

Jonathon's easy manner helped calm Samuel's nerves. "That's a good philosophy," he said.

And just like that they were in the kitchen and Cheri was hugging him the second he walked through the door. "Oh, Samuel, I haven't had the chance to speak to you all day. And honestly, I don't even know what to say to you. It must be so hard."

Hard for him? Samuel was baffled. *Cheri was worried about how he felt?* But, then again, that was Cheri. That was Thad. They were always thinking about others. No wonder their marriage had lasted. Maybe that was why his hadn't. He did have a tendency to focus on his own needs.

"Don't worry about me, Cheri, I'm here for you." Samuel responded with more courage than he felt. "Thad wouldn't leave us stranded here on the trail if we couldn't find our way."

Cheri took a step back, her hands still clutching Samuel's arms. She positively beamed. "That's why he loved you, Samuel. You understood him so well."

Samuel blushed from the attention.

"I think you know everyone here," Cheri said.

Samuel did know everyone in some small way. Cheri, Sarah, Jonathon and his wife Marie, their children Michael and Lauren, Ben and Father Langston. Samuel stepped over to the kitchen counter and shook Father Langston's hand to introduce himself, and that's when he saw it.

The urn. The simple silver urn that had been on the altar. Thad. His ashes.

Samuel jerked his gaze away, and everybody in the room

saw it. Cheri was closest and moved to his side to take his arm again. "Sorry, Samuel. It's kind of a shock at first, but we've been moving Thad around the house for days. First, we had him on top of the piano. Then in the family room. Now, the kitchen. I hope you don't find that too morbid."

"Cheri, I'm sure Samuel knows that Thad didn't like to stand still for too long," Sarah piped in. Jonathon laughed in response.

"Since the subject has been so indelicately broached, I think I'll get right to it," Cheri said. "It's actually why I'm glad you were able to come back tonight. We need to find a final resting place for Thad. I don't have to tell any of you that he died so suddenly that I don't know for certain if Thad had a final preference.

"I won't pretend we didn't have some conversations about how we would deal with things when one of us died. We'd joke at times, but it was pretty clear Thad preferred cremation because he used to tell me all the interesting ways I could deal with his 'dust' when the time came. Like send him into space, have him made into a diamond pendant or place him inside a statue."

"I'd vote for putting him into orbit," Michael interjected enthusiastically. "That'd be awesome."

"It would be, Michael. And your grandpa would enjoy that ride to outer space, I'm sure. But I think it'd make me dizzy thinking about him going round and round the earth so fast," Cheri said with a sad smile. "You know, the thing that Thad said most often to me was that I should just throw his ashes to the wind on top of a mountain of my choosing. That seems to make the most sense. My problem is what mountain?"

"Mount Everest?" Lauren suggested, not be outdone by her brother.

Cheri walked to her granddaughter and bent down to kiss her cheek. "Another good idea, Sweetie, but I want to be able to go—for us all to go—to say this last goodbye to Grandpa. I don't think I could make it all the way up the tallest mountain in the world."

"I would help you, Grandma," offered Lauren, pleading.

"I know you would, Lauren, but your dad and Aunt Sarah and I have been discussing this for the last few days, and we think we know just the place Grandpa would've chosen if he'd had the opportunity to tell us." Cheri turned to face Samuel. "Now, Samuel, I don't want to put you on the spot, but this is just one way to check that Jonathon, Sarah and I have it right."

"I'm sure you do already," said Samuel feeling the pressure again at being the center of unwanted attention.

"Just think for a moment of a place, other than this house, that you connect the most with Thad. Where would that be?" Cheri asked.

The question held all the pressure of a final exam. A true test of his friendship with Thad. Samuel's mind instantly went blank. Then he closed his eyes and pictured Thad. On a mountaintop. His hair buffeted by the breeze, his face turned to the setting sun with that mischievous grin. Too easy. Way too easy.

He opened his eyes and mouth at the same time.

"Sahalie."

Ashes and Elders

AS THE 9:35 FERRY CARRIED SAMUEL BACK TO Seattle, he kept replaying the conversation in Thad's kitchen. *Sahalie*. It made perfect sense. That was where Thad—and Sarah—had cut their teeth on the outdoors. It's where Thad and he had begun many of their backpacking trips into the Cascade Mountains. Thad's grandfather had built a small log cabin at a bend on the Salmon la Sac River about four rugged miles below Cooper Lake. The place hadn't changed much in almost ninety years. No indoor plumbing. No electricity. Just oil lamps and candles. A massive fireplace and hearth and an old nickel-plated beauty of a stove. Going there was like turning back the clock.

Thad and his family referred to the cabin as Sahalie, but that was because of its proximity to the mountain. It wasn't a big mountain, as far as mountains go in the Cascades. It wasn't that difficult of a climb, though there was a steep, exposed section near the top. It was the view from Sahalie. This peak wasn't carved from wind or water; it was shaped by sunsets. When the sun went down, Cooper Lake became a golden pool that spilled its shimmering wealth down the whole length of the river and set the valley glowing. The first time Samuel watched a sunset from the top of Sahalie, he knew exactly what people meant when they said they'd had an intense spiritual experience. The peak was like Mother Nature's Chartres, a cathedral of the soul.

Samuel knew it was the perfect place to spread Thad's ashes. But that wasn't the question on his mind as the ferry churned its way towards the bright lights of the Seattle waterfront. He was questioning his role in the process. In the kitchen just hours ago, they had tried to work out the plan. All of them realized that the cabin and Sahalie itself wouldn't be accessible until the late spring. Mid-May was probably the earliest they could plan to make the trip. And then there were all the complications of who could go when. The biggest concern was over Jonathon's daughter Lauren, who was scheduled to leave on a Youth Ambassadors Abroad trip to Australia and New Zealand. Marie was chaperoning. They'd be gone from mid-May to the end of July.

Sarah was scheduled to be gone August through mid-October on a ten-week European vacation she'd been planning for years. She'd even talked to Cheri about joining her for part of it to help her in the aftermath of Thad's death. The group had been in a quandary. There wasn't much of a window for all of them to be there.

It was Marie who'd helped them figure it out. "I think it makes the most sense to take Thad up to Sahalie over

Memorial Day. Lauren and I won't be able to be there, but we'll be there in spirit. Jonathon can take pictures for us. Memorial Day just seems so fitting."

Jonathon had hugged his wife close. "Thanks for offering to do that." He turned to his daughter, "What about you, pumpkin? Is that all right with you?"

"But I want to be with you to say goodbye to Grandpa," Lauren said disappointedly.

Cheri went to her granddaughter and put her arms around her. "I think I know how you can help us out. Grandpa always wanted to see Australia. Would you be willing to spread some of his ashes on your trip? That way Grandpa will have made it Down Under."

Lauren eyes had brightened. "Yes. That would make him happy."

There had been a palpable sense of relief at the decision about when to go to Sahalie. Then—at least to Samuel's way of thinking—Cheri dropped a bit of a bombshell. She explained that part of her motivation for finding a place to spread Thad's ashes was so Ben and some members of his Eldering group could posthumously perform the Eldering Ceremony for Thad. She asked Ben to explain.

In his humble way, Ben did. He told them the ceremony was not long or religious. It was intended to acknowledge the contributions of the new Elder. Ben said that he, Father Langston and Fawn Well, a much respected Elder, who had all helped in mentoring Thad, planned to go to Sahalie to honor Cheri's husband in this way.

Jonathon and Marie immediately thanked Ben and Father Langston for their willingness to do this for Thad and Cheri. During that exchange, Samuel had looked over at Sarah, who had remained silent while Ben was speaking. Sarah caught his eye, and he could tell she had some reservations. It was as if she felt the same gnawing question: *Who are these Eldering people who are claiming my brother as one of their own?*

That was one of the questions Samuel wrestled with on the ferry back to Seattle. The other more immediate question was much more painful. Literally. The Morton's neuroma in his right foot was killing him. These last few months it'd been flaring up more often and more intensely. How was he going to hike up Sahalie if his condition worsened?

He knew he needed to get in better shape, but his neuroma was keeping him off his feet. It was a Catch-22. On top of that, tax season was gearing up. He was going to be slammed through the end of April. On one level, he welcomed the business and the distraction from Thad's death. On the other hand, Ben Broader had told him that he needed to make some changes in his attitude and lifestyle if he was ever going to understand why Thad had wanted to become an Elder.

Once again, his buddy Thad had launched him on a reluctant journey. This one, though, presented many more questions—and there was much more at stake. Could he grind this one out alone? He closed his eyes and pictured his friend. The smile. The careless confidence.

Maybe he didn't have to do this alone. Samuel reached into his pocket for the card he'd been given right before he left Cheri's. On the bottom was a phone number. On the top, the card simply read:

Ben Broader
Elder

A Step Forward

TWO STEPS BACK. THAT'S HOW SAMUEL FELT THE morning after Thad's funeral. His head hurt, his foot ached and his thinking was thicker than the February fog gathered outside.

Not a great night's sleep, up three times to the bathroom, but Samuel had knuckled down and met with all his scheduled clients that morning. By mid-afternoon, he knew he had to give into his body's exhaustion. He drove home, flopped down on his couch and fell soundly asleep. He woke two hours later feeling better. He got himself a bite to eat and then sat down with a legal pad and pen, thinking about Cheri's plan to spread Thad's ashes.

If he was going to commit to Mt. Sahalie, he had to start exercising. He'd always been active when it came to summer hiking with Thad, but the rest of the year was hit or miss. Usually miss. He needed to change that. But he also had to be careful of his foot. Since the initial diagnosis of the Morton's neuroma years ago, he'd been given several different options. The only suggestion Samuel had followed was buying shoes with bigger toe boxes and over-the-counter arch supports. He couldn't afford the time or expense of surgery on the neuroma, but now it might be worthwhile trying a series of cortisone shots and perhaps springing for some customized orthotic inserts. He just couldn't let the almost continual discomfort and increasingly immobilizing flare-ups wear him down.

Plus, he needed to get in much better shape. In a low-impact way. Two ideas came to mind: swimming and biking. He didn't own a bike and western Washington didn't have the greatest biking weather, though the city of Redmond fancied itself the biking capital of the world. However, if he joined a health club, he could ride stationery bikes and also swim if he found a club with a pool.

The only thing nagging him was the expense. Could he afford it? But, then again, could he afford not to deal with some of his health issues head on? It was the same old conundrum. People generally knew what was good for them—eat right, exercise daily—yet how many did it consistently? Knowledge and action didn't always go hand in hand.

That reminded Samuel of something Ben had told him at the coffee shop yesterday. He'd said that a clear purpose was the key to committing to a course of action. Samuel knew it was in his best interest to get in shape, yet he was finding all kinds of excuses to not change his sedentary routine. And now he felt a stronger sense of urgency because of Thad's death. He had to be able to climb Sahalie and spread his ashes. That was the way to honor their long friendship. The sense of purpose was clear. He had to go with Cheri, Jonathon, Michael, Sarah, Ben and the others. He had to find a way to do it.

He booted up his computer and searched health clubs in the Redmond area. There were more than he anticipated, though one search result immediately stood out, and he mentally kicked himself for not thinking of it before. The Northshore YMCA. It was only a few miles away. He drove by it a few times a week. He checked out their website. Only $26 a month for seniors. Samuel had a hard time thinking of himself as a 'senior.' *Might as well start benefiting from the discounts*, he reasoned. And this Y had a pool as well.

He congratulated himself on taking an important step. He could go in to the Y tomorrow, sign up and find out what programs might best fit his needs. Satisfied, he closed the browser window on his computer and there, staring back at him on the screen, was his grandson Jimmy. His son David had sent him the picture about a month ago and Samuel had decided to use it as the background on his computer screen. Jimmy was decked out in his Spiderman pajamas with a red towel as a cape safety pinned around his neck. In one hand he held a Nerf light saber, but what made Samuel smile the most was what he wore on his head. It was a classic beanie with a propeller on the top that Samuel had bought him at the State Fair last August. It had been a wonderful day of corn dogs, pig petting, scones and ring toss.

Purpose. Did Samuel really have to look far for that? He scolded himself for ever wondering what he had to live for. *He had family he loved.* He couldn't allow himself to forget that anymore, even in the middle of the day-to-day concerns of running his business and dealing with health issues. He had more than enough motivation to keep himself going—if he could keep his family and friends front and center. For a moment, Samuel felt a small sliver of what it meant to be an Elder.

Ben Broader had told him that Elders believed the key is to live for others, to give of oneself. Maybe it *was* possible for him.

He savored the picture of his grandson for a few more moments. Then he got up, deciding to drive to the Y this evening. He had a clear purpose. Now he had to commit and not put things off. He grabbed his wallet and keys and took a confident step towards the door.

Then he stopped abruptly.

What was he doing? Exactly where were his priorities? He needed to consider what was really important in his life. It was clear that Jimmy and Thad were. But what about his son, David? Their relationship needed as much work as his aching and tired body did. He needed to take a step in that direction too.

With a quick about-face, he went to the phone to call his son and say "Hi" and talk to Jimmy too. Then he'd go to the Y and commit to becoming stronger and fitter with his son and grandson clearly in mind. Along with Thad, whose memory kept pushing him forward one step at a time.

BEN THERE

OVER A MONTH LATER ON A SUNDAY AFTERNOON, Samuel was sitting on his couch, head down. His coffee table and kitchen counter were strewn with documents and folders. Tax Day, April 15th, was less than two weeks away and he was swamped and exhausted. It was like the third day of a fifty-mile hike when you know you have an entire day of steep elevation gain ahead of you. Switchback after switchback. One foot in front of the other. Grind time.

He wanted to just close his eyes and let his leaden limbs and heavy thoughts sink into the dark void of sleep. He felt like he deserved it after how hard he'd been working—not only at his business, but also at getting in shape. He'd been disciplined about going to the Y at least every other day, and he was beginning to see some results. He wished he could chalk it all up to his own will power, but he knew that Rolf had a lot to do with it.

He'd met Rolf during his third swim. Pacing himself evenly for about 20 minutes, he'd felt decent. Rolf was getting out of the pool the same time as Samuel and they almost bumped into each other. Samuel had apologized. The tall, lanky man with a shock of closely trimmed white hair had simply said in reply, "No worries. At my age, bumping into things reassures me that I'm not dreaming—or worse."

Samuel had laughed. Rolf had introduced himself and asked if Samuel had been swimming there long. When Samuel told him he'd just started, Rolf mentioned, "Well, this is a good time for swimming. Always seems to be less crowded—and the lifeguards are cuter." He'd made the last point as a plain statement of fact. No wink or nod. Just how Rolf saw things.

So Samuel started swimming at that same time, and he and Rolf would usually chat for a few minutes after their laps. Rolf was 79, but he looked twice as fit as Samuel. When Samuel asked him for his secret, Rolf, matter-of-fact as always, explained, "I'm Norwegian. We eat a lot of fish, and we can't stand still."

Rolf's example motivated Samuel to work out on a regular basis. In his mind, he called it 'no excuse' time: it was just another version of 'grind time.' However, on this particular Sunday afternoon, with a boatload of work and his body feeling heavy and sore, he was thinking about skipping his evening swim. *What would Rolf say?* Probably nothing. Though friendly, he seemed to be a pretty detached observer of the world around him. *What about Thad?* That was easy. "Come on, Blockhead. Get off your butt and get moving!"

Samuel smiled. The image of Ben Broader popped into his mind and he wondered what Ben would tell him about feeling sorry for himself and making excuses. Curiously, Samuel really wanted to know. He wasn't at all sure this wasn't a subconscious ploy on his part to put off going to the Y, but he lifted his tired self off the couch and went to search through the small bowl of business cards by the phone.

The simple card Ben had given him after Thad's funeral was right on top. He picked it up. *Ben Broader. Elder.* He considered that title: Elder. *What had being an Elder really done for Thad? And what could it do for him?*

He dialed the phone. Ben answered on the fourth ring.

"Hello, Ben. This is Samuel Block. We met at Thad's funeral and you gave me your card. I was just calling...." Samuel halted, trying to think of why he'd really called. It suddenly seemed foolish to be asking about Eldering. "I was just calling to ask how the plans to spread Thad's ashes were going. I didn't want to bother Cheri about it, but thought you might know something."

"It's good to hear from you, Samuel," Ben said brightly. "I'm glad you called. We're still on for Memorial Day weekend, but Father Langston won't be able to make it. He broke his collarbone."

"His collarbone? Oh, ouch. How's he doing? Was it a fall?" Samuel conjured up the classic senior scenario: old person falls in shower and breaks leg or hip or wrist. Bad balance and brittle bones. Samuel knew those days lay ahead for him.

"Jack is doing fine. He was up at Snoqualmie Pass last Saturday and took a spill. I guess the snow was a little mushy. He's been skiing for 60 years and he's excellent, but he wanted to give snowboarding a try. Said he thought he was getting the hang of it on the bunny slope, and so he went up on an intermediate run. That's where he learned that taking a fall on skis is much different than on a snowboard. I think his pride hurts him more than anything."

"But that's a tough injury—at any age. I hope he's taking it well."

"Jack is not the kind of person to get down about things. He's only sorry he won't be able to join us to help spread Thad's ashes and participate in the Eldering Ceremony on Sahalie. I think you would've enjoyed getting to know him better."

"How old is he?" Samuel couldn't help asking. He still felt the odd need to compare his situation to those around him.

"He's 73, but he's in good shape," Ben answered.

"That's impressive he still skis—and actually wanted to try snowboarding. I hope this injury doesn't end his days on the slopes."

"That's unlikely. Jack'll work on getting back to skiing. It'll take time, but that's one of the advantages to being older. We've usually learned that rushing things often leads to more setbacks. We know that, as we age, physical stuff happens to us. For me, it's my cholesterol, my heart and I've got a bum knee too. But to have the circumstances of your health rule your life is a big mistake. It's how you relate to what's happening with your body that's important. Choosing to be 'well,' no matter what you're dealing with, can help you find the courage and the strength to make things work. As with most challenges in life, it's your attitude that makes the difference."

"And your health plan coverage," Samuel interjected sarcastically.

"You're right about that," Ben admitted. "But, as I've told you before, health and well-being are not the same thing. They are complementary, but you have to attend to both. Managing your health as you age doesn't mean you just turn your body over to a physician when something goes wrong. And developing a sense of well-being doesn't come from therapy sessions. Like most things in life, you have to work at them."

Samuel thought about Rolf's comment about Norwegians not standing still. "I guess we all know you have to work hard at things in order to improve, but it doesn't always translate into action."

"Actually," Ben responded, "you'd be surprised at how many people don't associate effort with results. Remember, we live in an age of lotteries, casinos and instant YouTube fame. A lot of folks think it's all about luck. That's why we stress purpose and perseverance in Eldering. The commitment to positive action will see you through, even if results seem slow in coming. You just have to stick to your beliefs and keep at it."

"Well, now I really feel like I can't skip out on swimming tonight!"

"Oh? Where do you go?" Ben asked.

"I've got a membership at the YMCA. I've been swimming and doing some light workouts, trying to get in shape for Memorial Day weekend."

"That's great, Samuel. I commend you. I'm not much of a swimmer—which is not something an old Navy seaman likes to admit—but I'm working out as well. I certainly don't want to have you young pups waiting for me on the trail, and I can't miss Thad's ceremony."

"I guess you'll be the *elder* statesman of the group," Samuel remarked, pleased at his little pun.

Ben laughed. "Actually, I won't. There'll be another Elder coming with us. She couldn't make it to Thad's funeral because she was out of the country. Her name is Fawn Well and I can only hope I'm as strong and feisty at the age of 87 as she is."

"I remember Cheri mentioning her name," Samuel said. "Wow. She's going to hike up Sahalie with us?"

"Once you meet Fawn, you'll quickly learn that nothing—and I mean *nothing*—stands in her way."

"She sounds impressive."

On the other end of the line, Ben whistled. "Just wait. I may have been Thad's official mentor in our Eldering group, but Fawn mentors all Elders. She inspires others to aspire. I think she had more to do with Thad wanting to become an Elder than I did. She has that impact on people."

In his mind, Samuel called up a picture of Mother Teresa. A wizened dynamo of faith and determination. "I look forward to meeting her," he said.

"She's someone you'll never forget," Ben promised.

"Well, thanks for the update, Ben. I better get going. Between you and Fawn, I've got a lot to live up to."

"Just remember to take one step at a time. We're not climbing Sahalie tomorrow," Ben advised.

"Will do. Thanks. Talk to you later," Samuel said and hung up. He surveyed the clutter of tax work spread around the condo. He sighed. Opening a diet cola, he dove into organizing all his work folders before going to the Y.

As he climbed out of the pool later that evening, he felt reinvigorated. He hadn't given into his weariness that afternoon, he'd stuck to his fitness plan and he'd actually kept up with Rolf for most of his swim. That felt good.

THE LONG AND WINDING ROAD

AS THEY ROLLED PAST MILEPOST 36, SAMUEL HAD a sense of déjà vu. He'd been here before many times. He was on I-90 heading east to Snoqualmie Pass and into the Cascade Mountains in Thad's Chevy Tahoe. He'd driven the highway with Thad many times, and milepost 36 marked the beginning of the real ascent into the mountains. He took a deep breath and let it out slowly.

Only this time Thad wasn't driving his car. Samuel was. Thad was in the silver urn packed tightly in the back with all their gear. Ashes and dust. It made Samuel want to pound the horn and scream to the world that it wasn't fair. Even if Thad had lived a good life and died almost painlessly. He was too young. Too vital.

Samuel gripped the steering wheel tighter and kept telling himself to breathe slowly. He couldn't lose it now. Cheri had asked him to drive when they'd picked him up.

That whole scene in itself had been surreal. Just like the last two months. Between tax season and trying to get himself fitter, Samuel had been in a strange place. An in-between place. He was too busy to be bored, but at the same time he felt like he wasn't doing anything he should be doing. Like a machine left running when the factory has been closed and abandoned.

The knowledge that he would be spreading Thad's ashes over Memorial Day gave him a sense of focus, but he still felt an emptiness. Even trying to stay more in touch with David and Jimmy didn't fill the void. He'd hoped that when the day finally came for the drive to Sahalie this strange numbness would have begun to fade. But when he came down from his condo with a full pack slung over his right shoulder and saw Thad's Tahoe, he almost broke down.

Did they think this trip would make up for all they'd lost? Their whole journey to spread Thad's ashes and hold an Eldering Ceremony on top of Sahalie felt like a puny gesture. Even though he'd been able to put on a good show on the outside, he was seething on the inside. Luckily for him, Ben had kept up the empty banter as they had headed out of Redmond, and by the time they'd reached North Bend, both Cheri and Sarah had fallen asleep in the back seat.

Samuel had been hoping Ben would fall asleep in the passenger seat as well, but he seemed content to study the scenery as it passed by. Samuel began hoping the trip would go fast. The plan was to pick up Fawn Well in Cle Elum around eleven, and then drive to the cabin where Jonathon and Michael would be waiting. Thad's son and grandson had driven up the night before to get the cabin ready, since no one in the family had been there since the late fall.

It was all going according to Cheri's plan, except that Samuel's state of mind robbed him of any meaningful purpose inside that plan. He drove on, trying to convince himself he could maintain his calm. Just grind it out. One step at a time.

Ben's questioned startled him. "How are you doing?" he asked.

Samuel quickly stole a glance at Ben, who looked relaxed and at ease in a flannel shirt and well-worn jeans and boots. "Fine," he responded as blandly as he could manage.

"You just seem a bit distracted. You want me to drive?"

Samuel tried to be light. "This isn't a Prius. This is a gas-sucking beast."

"Oh, I know something about those. I owned a Hummer for a while."

"A Hummer? What were you thinking?" Samuel asked, intrigued.

"I guess it was my second mid-life crisis. It was after Darlene died, and I got nostalgic. I think the Hummer was my attempt to re-enlist." Ben chuckled softly.

"I remember you said you were in the Navy, on a submarine. Weren't you tempted to get a boat instead?"

"Oh, I've had a few in my day, but I did so much traveling for work that I'm sure barnacles spent a lot more time on my boats than I ever did."

In spite of himself, Samuel laughed at the remark. For some strange reason, his natural inclination was to resist

Ben's obvious attempts to build camaraderie, but Ben's easy manner and wit chipped away at his defensiveness.

"Why'd you do so much traveling?" Samuel asked.

"First it was sales, and then, because I was good at it, I became a manager. Then after a while I began consulting small businesses. I even worked with a couple of large corporations. I kind of approached my business career like the war."

"What do you mean?"

"It was all out. Competitive. Conquest. In the Navy, I was in combat and, as anyone who has ever been in combat knows, it can be both terrifying and exhilarating at the same time. It's the kind of adrenalin rush that comes when you've got a lot at stake, when every moment might be your last. It is being fully alive, fully present, fully in the 'now.'"

Ben paused for a moment. "It's so strange. I hated combat, never wanted to ever experience it again, but that exhilaration of putting yourself on the line, that's what drove me to win at business."

"Kind of like climbing a mountain," Samuel said with a nod of understanding.

"Yes," Ben agreed. "I think we all look for ways to keep feeling that 'aliveness'—that living on the edge."

Samuel changed lanes and accelerated the Tahoe past a semi struggling up the ever-steepening highway. He couldn't help thinking of himself as that lumbering truck.

"That's not what I've been feeling the last few years," Samuel confided, surprised by his own frankness. "I don't think I could be any further from that 'aliveness.' Health concerns. Loneliness. Bills. Debt. Not exactly exhilarating stuff."

Ben turned in his passenger seat, sensing the invitation in Samuel's admission. "I've come to believe the older we get, the more we realize that our life depends on recapturing that sense of exhilaration. In a way, each day is challenging us to see if we're still alive and engaged—or if we've just drifted to the sidelines to become spectators."

Samuel knowingly took the bait. "Is that another part of Eldering?"

"It's a big part of it. Eldering is one way of rethinking who we are and what is possible. It's about having the end of our lives be as filled with possibility as the beginning. You know, having the rest of your life be the best of your life. Eldering is also about wisdom and discovering how we can share what we've learned throughout our lives with others, making their lives better. Ultimately Eldering is about the kind of legacy you want to leave behind."

"You looking for a statue, Ben? Or maybe a Ben Broader Day?"

"I hadn't been thinking in those terms, exactly." Ben smiled. "Though I have always been fond of parades."

"Seventy-six trombones?"

"That'd do. You know, I don't care if people remember me specifically, but I'd like my spirit of wanting to make things better to be remembered. If I can pass along that positive energy, that exhilaration for life, that sense of renewal, then that's a good legacy.

"George Bernard Shaw once said he wanted to be 'used up' when he died. He didn't want to leave any of himself behind. I take that to mean he wanted to spend all his energy, all his talent, all his potential. To not leave any purpose unfulfilled. No regrets."

"Everybody has regrets," Samuel interjected, sure of himself on this point. He was certain he had enough for two lifetimes.

"Most do," Ben acknowledged. "But regrets, like all the indignities or injustices we perceive in life—all the 'slings and arrows of outrageous fortune' we think we suffer—don't have to follow us to our graves. We have the power to bury those historical hurts long before they're buried with us."

"You're waxing eloquent, Ben."

"And you're tailgating."

Samuel realized Ben was right and he eased up on the gas to widen the distance between the Tahoe and the mini-van in front. "Sorry. You really do speak well. I just tend to be sarcastic. Always have been. Thad used to call me *pes-Sam-mistic.*"

"No need to apologize. The real issue is where does that lead? If you see the future as dark and unfulfilling, that makes aging even tougher. With that negative perspective, you tend to either become a crank or a curmudgeon."

"I hope I'm leaning towards curmudgeon," Samuel said. "Maybe even a cuddly one."

Ben smiled. "I think that's possible. You aren't as negative as you seem to yourself, Samuel. I've had my bouts of negativity, even depression. Especially after Darlene died. The key is the broader outlook."

Samuel laughed. "The *Ben Broader* outlook?"

"Okay. I deserved that one. I'm not trying to trademark anything here. But, you know, just take a second to admire the view right out the windshield."

Samuel did a 180-degree scan. They were on the final approach to Snoqualmie Pass, coming up on Alpental, one of three ski resorts in the area. Mountains soared skyward on both sides of the highway. Snowfields sparkled in the sunlight, reaching up to craggy peaks. An impressive, almost mystical gateway into the Cascades.

"I guess it does pay to stop and smell the roses," Samuel admitted.

"Exactly. That's how you begin to change things. You make yourself get outside. Take the time to leave the dark house. Look around. Remember what the world has to offer—and pretty soon you begin to realize you have a lot to offer the world too."

"So I just need to do more hiking to become an Elder?"

"Getting outside more doesn't mean the outdoors. It means getting outside your routine—if it's become too narrow or too limiting. Getting outside your comfort zone to try new things and meet new people. It's about continued growth and giving back."

"The 'wisdom of the ages' and all that? I don't feel like I've really got many answers," Samuel lamented.

"But you've got experience. Vast amounts of it. How to run a business. How to climb a mountain. How to get through the death of a friend. You're not trying to spread eternal truths or lay down various 'good-old-days' laws. You're helping other people with the same kind of challenges you've faced at one time or another. Because of our age, we see the world differently. We hold a longer view, a more far-reaching time horizon. That can be a gift to other generations."

"Or a curse."

"You're sounding like that crusty curmudgeon already."

"What if that's just my honest perspective?" Samuel argued, testing Ben. "What if that's all I have to offer?"

Ben let out an uncharacteristic sigh. "Then heaven help you in an hour when you meet Fawn."

A chill ran down Samuel's spine. They remained silent. The Tahoe had reached the high point of the pass. It was downhill now. Samuel wondered just how far downhill he might personally skid on the rest of this journey. Reflexively, he put his foot over the brake. Playing it safe.

FAWN

SAMUEL'S NEUROMA, WHICH HADN'T FLARED UP badly for over a month, was the first thing he felt when he stepped out of the SUV at Cle Elum. He winced and leaned on the open door.

"Get a crick from driving?" Sarah asked. She'd been the first to hop out of the Tahoe when they arrived at the small market that served as the town's hub. She was rubbing her lower back. "A long drive is a surefire way to get my muscles tight and sore."

"Yeah, I'm sure someday just breathing will make me feel like an NFL halfback after a rough game," Samuel replied, trying to play it tough.

"Here, let me try something that might help," Sarah offered. "Where's it hurt most?"

"You name it," Samuel bantered, not wanting to identify the neuroma. He didn't want anyone thinking he might hold them back during the climb tomorrow.

She came over and took his right hand in both of hers.

"Well, then I'll try my palm panacea for you." She began to lightly and methodically massage his palm with her thumbs and then gently pull along each finger.

Samuel was amazed at how her simple motions in his one hand radiated outward through his body. The effect was almost immediate. Tension left him and he felt relaxed and warm. A wonderful sense of well-being filled him as he watched her hands on his. Almost bashfully, he glanced up at her face. She was completely focused on his hands, like they were the only thing in the world. Again, a thrill went through Samuel's body. Something he hadn't felt in a long time.

"How do you feel now?" Sarah asked as she released his hand.

"Much better," Samuel responded with a smile. And it was true. He felt much more relaxed and re-energized. Though he still felt the discomfort of the neuroma in his right foot, he knew it wasn't going to be a full-blown flare-up. "Where'd you learn to do that?"

"Took a few classes. I was in a car accident about twenty years ago. I had severe neck pain and massage therapy was part of my treatment. It really opened my eyes to how massage can help the body heal and recover."

"Well, that hand massage is an eye opener. I bet with that trick, you make friends easily," Samuel teased.

Sarah smiled slyly. "Oh, that's nothing compared to my ear massage."

Samuel felt himself blushing and covered it with a hearty laugh. "I'll bet. If I sprain my earlobe on the way up Sahalie, I'll know who to call."

Sarah laughed, and Cheri called out from the other side of the Tahoe. "Hey, you two, enough merriment. We've got to pick up a few things before Fawn gets here. Samuel, will you grab two bags of ice? Sarah and I'll pay for them inside when we get the ribs for tonight."

"No problem," Samuel called back. As he walked over to the ice machine at the far end of the market, he took a deep breath. The rich scent of Douglas fir and the clean blue skies above lifted his spirits as much as Sarah's gentle touch. He hadn't felt this good in a long time. Maybe he didn't have to worry about bringing the group down with his negative outlook. Maybe this was one of those moments Ben had just been talking about. Maybe there was a brighter side he could embrace.

His heart much lighter than it had been all morning, he carried the ice back to the tailgate of the Tahoe. He was loading the bags into an empty cooler when he heard Ben's voice a little way off. Samuel turned to see Ben talking into the passenger side of an older VW bus in meticulous condition. After a moment or two, Ben stepped back and the passenger door opened.

A diminutive woman stepped out. She wore jeans and a simple white blouse with the sleeves rolled up to the elbows. Her long grey hair hung down her back in a single braid. Her face was bronze and finely creased. She reached back into the VW and pulled out a well-worn backpack.

Ben didn't offer to take it from her. Instead he gestured towards the Tahoe and Samuel standing at the open tailgate. Samuel could see the woman focus her attention sharply on him. They walked briskly over, and Ben said as they arrived, "Fawn, this is Samuel Block, one of Thad's oldest and closest friends. Samuel, this is Fawn Well."

Samuel extended his hand. "Very pleased to meet you, Ms. Well."

Fawn took his hand. And if Samuel was surprised by the firmness of her grip, he was even more surprised by her silence. She locked on his eyes in a most disconcerting way, as if assessing his worthiness to call himself a friend of Thad. Her gaze was like the ice he'd just stowed in the car and Samuel felt his sense of warmth and well-being freeze back into glacial inadequacy. This was a person who knew people. Could gaze into their being, plumb their soul.

Fawn gave the slightest of nods, releasing her grip. She handed Samuel her backpack, then turned and walked towards the market. Ben followed her.

Samuel held Fawn's backpack. It was light and smelled of pine and smoke. He gingerly placed it on top of the other bags. Then he reached for his own bag. He dug until he found his toilet kit. He rummaged through his blood pressure and prostate medications and found his bottle of ibuprofen. He wrestled with the safety cap and then downed two of the little red pills.

Meeting Fawn Well was unsettling, as Ben had forewarned. Samuel felt tense. The pain of his neuroma had flared. This small Native American woman, with one look, had completely flustered him. Samuel felt—even though he didn't take much stock in folk tales—that Fawn had given him the evil eye.

CABIN FEVER

SAMUEL DROVE THE 35 MILES TO THE CABIN AS IF
he were a chauffeur. Not permitted to speak unless spoken
to. Fawn sat in the back with Cheri and Sarah. Cheri filled
Sarah in on Fawn's responsibilities as the President of the
Quinault Indian Nation. She'd been appointed by the gov-
ernor in 2002 and worked to manage the resources of the
various coastal tribes living on the reservation.

After listening to Cheri's account, Sarah said to Fawn,
"You must be so busy."

"Yes, there are always needs," Fawn explained. "I am
just coming back from a forum on the Yakama Reservation
concerning what we can do about the high dropout rate
from school among our young people. It's a very big problem. We as a people have a lot of problems, but we've got to
solve them. We owe it to our youth."

"I'm so grateful you found the time to come with us…"
Sarah paused, not quite sure how to finish her thought,
"…and put Thad to rest."

"It is a privilege for me. And I don't believe Thad will ever rest. He will continue to work with us. His is a strong spirit. As strong as they come," Fawn told them with a gentle certainty.

Samuel could only imagine how insubstantial his own spirit would be in comparison. He drove on, trying to appreciate the beauty of the day and the approach to the cabin along Cle Elum Lake.

By the time they pulled into the narrow, winding drive that led to the cabin, his spirits had revived a bit. When he saw the cabin, he felt an immediate surge of warmth and familiarity. The bright Scandinavian blue of the window frames and shutters contrasting with the weathered grey logs. The steeply pitched aluminum roof glinting bright silver in the sunlight. Best of all, the front porch with its Adirondack chairs perched twenty feet above the Salmon la Sac River as it flowed right past the cabin and then abruptly turned at the base of a spectacular buttress of granite that provided the cabin its unique setting.

The river was coursing full and swift with the spring run-off and its roar was audible inside the Tahoe. Samuel opened his door and hurriedly stepped out of the car. He went straight onto the porch and looked down into the cascading river, frothy and alive. The screen door shot open and Michael bounded out.

"Uncle Sam! You're here. Wanna play some horseshoes?"

Smiling broadly, Samuel answered, "What? You're old enough to throw horseshoes?"

"I'm almost 10, Uncle Sam!"

"Okay, then, Michael, you're on!"

Jonathon stepped out onto the front porch and shook Samuel's hand. Then he turned to his son. "Michael, let's help everyone unload the car first and then we can toss some shoes."

Michael jumped off the porch and sprinted down to the Tahoe. Samuel followed along with Jonathon. Ben introduced Fawn to Michael and Jonathon. Samuel paid special attention to how she looked into their eyes. Her eyes lit up as she shook Michael's hand. "Pleased to meet you, Michael. You have your grandfather's eyes. Strong. Bright."

Michael beamed and loaded himself with bags to take into the cabin. Samuel grabbed his things and followed Michael in. Nothing in the cabin had changed. Nothing needed to. Right inside the front door was the main living area. A massive river rock fireplace and hearth was at the center of the cabin. A worn leather couch and four rocking chairs surrounded the hearth. To the left ran a long pine table with benches set in front of large windows. At the far end of the table, the kitchen began and then swung to the right behind the fireplace. Pine cabinets, an L-shaped laminate counter and the nickel-plated stove butted up to the back of the fireplace. Simplicity at its best.

To the right of the doorway was another couch along the wall that ended in a stairway with a hairpin turn going up to the sleeping loft. A slow, hot fire was burning in the fireplace. Samuel knew how the stones of the broad hearth, once they got warm, would radiate heat throughout the cabin and keep it snug during their stay. He slowly climbed the steep stairway, making a mental note to be extra careful, something he'd not worried a whole lot about when he visited in younger days.

Upstairs, the cabin was divided into three sleeping areas. The chimney rose through the center of the room. Nestled on each side of the chimney were rows of narrow metal bed-frames with bare mattresses that brushed the bottom edge of the steeply pitched roof. Floral print curtains that could be drawn around the beds on one side designated the girls' area. Striped curtains designated the boys'. At the front end of the cabin was an outside sleeping porch.

That was where Samuel headed. The porch had four beds. Two on either side of the door. This is where he'd always slept, because he loved going to sleep to the roar of the river just below him. He placed his pack and sleeping bag on the far bed to the left, noticing that neither Jonathon nor Michael's gear was on any of the other beds. Samuel kind of hoped that he might be the only one who wanted to sleep out here. He'd been living by himself for so long he'd gotten used to sleeping alone. As much as he dreaded the isolation that could come with aging, he liked his personal privacy.

He pulled his sleeping bag out of the stuff bag and stretched it out on the bed. He put his watch and condo keys into the outside pocket of his daypack. It felt good to leave those things behind. That was what Sahalie was all about—not only turning back the clock, but also forgetting it for a while. Thad had told him once that his grandfather, who had built the cabin decades before, referred to the days he spent here as 'sacred.' Looking out onto the rush and crash of the river below, Samuel had to agree. This place was sacred to him as well.

As Samuel turned to go back and help finish emptying the Tahoe, the door swung open and Fawn came out onto the sleeping porch. She looked around in her discerning manner, stepped to the high railing and looked out over the river. She threw her pack on the bed farthest from Samuel's. As she turned to go back through the door, she said with no particular emotion, "I'm hoping you don't snore louder than the river."

When she'd left, Samuel sat down on his bed and sighed, considering whether he should move his stuff inside. It was obvious Fawn didn't like him. Was she trying to provoke him? After a few moments, he stood, resolved to avoid her as much as possible. She was more the stranger here than he was. She was the outsider. He could play her game of mutual indifference. He was here for Thad and the others, not for Fawn Well.

He hurried back downstairs and helped haul the ice and coolers around to the back of the cabin where there was a covered porch and cold room. As he was finishing the last load, he heard the familiar clink of iron hitting iron. He walked down the little path leading away from the back of the cabin. About thirty feet from the back door, the path split. To the right was the outhouse, another fifty feet away.

Samuel took the left path through a stand of vine maples which emptied onto a good-sized oval clearing.

Michael was poised at one end of the horseshoe pit with one of the horseshoes in his hand. Samuel did a double take. Michael's grip and form were exactly like his grandfather's. It was as if he were watching Thad as a young man.

Michael saw him and yelled, "You ready, Uncle Sam?"

Samuel went over to the log bench and picked up the other set of shoes. "You bet I am, Michael. This is just what I need."

And indeed it was. Samuel easily won the first game and then let Michael win the second. It's just what Thad would've done. Let someone know that winning is always possible.

ROCKING THE BOAT

AFTER HORSESHOES, SAMUEL AND MICHAEL WENT back to the cabin and had lunch with the others. The day had warmed up considerably, so Jonathon pulled some camp chairs out of the storage shed on the far side of the cabin. He set them out on the expansive granite outcropping that tapered in a series of cascading steps to the river's edge about sixty feet downriver.

Cheri, Jonathon and Sarah traded stories about swimming and floating down the river. Their recollections mostly revolved around how cold the river was most of the year.

Samuel had a story of his own. He told them of a day in early September when he and Thad, in their early twenties, had tried to walk the riverbank the entire three miles up to Cooper Lake. The river had been unusually low that summer, so they thought they had a shot at it. They got within a half mile when they encountered Ron's Canyon.

According to Thad, his family called it Ron's Canyon after a friend of his grandfather's who claimed he'd made it through to Cooper Lake. If he had, then Samuel knew he deserved to have his name attached to that narrow gorge which snaked for a quarter mile through precipitous walls of stone and a non-stop series of sluice-like waterfalls. Samuel and Thad had packed along fins and life jackets, but the current was too swift, the rocks too slick and the water in that sunless stretch too cold. They'd turned back about a third of the way through the canyon, joking that Ron must've been half salmon to make it through.

As they finished up with lunch, Michael asked his dad if they could go canoeing on Cooper Lake. "That sounds like a good idea," Jonathon replied. "Especially since it looks like it's going to be warm this afternoon. Anyone want to join us?"

"Are you thinking of driving or taking the trail?" Sarah asked.

Samuel knew it was a meandering four-mile trail to the lake. It was a beautiful hike, but he didn't want to overdo it before the climb tomorrow.

"I'm thinking we'll drive," Jonathon said.

"Then I'm in," Sarah said.

That seemed to be the consensus, though Fawn said she wanted to take the trail and would join them at the lake. They cleaned up, and then threw their gear into both cars for the drive. Samuel hadn't been up to Cooper Lake in close to fifteen years and it was like hooking back up with an old friend. The lake, some three miles long and a mile wide, was ringed by thick stands of Douglas fir. At the north end of the lake, Glacier Peak rose like a brilliant snow cone. And because no powerboats were allowed, it was quiet and serene.

There was only one parking area at the south end of the lake, near where the trail from the cabin let out. While Cheri and Ben got out the camp chairs and set them up at the water's edge, Jonathon, Michael, Sarah and Samuel tramped to the nearest cabin. Thad's folks had known the family who owned the property for over fifty years. They let the Curtis family keep their two canoes chained to a tree near the water.

Jonathon unlocked the boats and he and Michael grabbed opposite ends of the faded blue one and started slowly towards the water. Sarah and Samuel hefted the other canoe, a forest green duplicate.

"These seemed so much lighter four decades ago," Samuel said with a wink.

"So was I," Sarah mused.

"Oh, you're looking fit. I'm the one who's added the ballast."

"I wouldn't say that. You seem to have trimmed up since I saw you in February," she said.

Samuel was pleased she noticed. "I started swimming. Had to do something so I wouldn't embarrass myself."

"Amen to that," Sarah chimed in.

They put the canoes partway in the water near the camp chairs and Jonathon collected the paddles and life jackets he'd brought from the cabin.

"How do we want to divide up?" Jonathon asked.

Michael wasn't shy. "I want to go with you and Aunt Sarah."

"Okay," Jonathon said, "that's one canoe."

Cheri announced from one of the camp chairs, "I think I'm just going to sit here, enjoy the sunshine and read my book."

"You mean you don't want to race us, Mom?" Jonathon teased.

"No!" she replied emphatically. "Your father goaded me into that once and we ended swimming one of those canoes back to shore. No tomfoolery out there."

"Tomfoolery," Jonathon snorted. "You make me feel like an irresponsible young whippersnapper."

Cheri looked at Ben with a wry smile and pointed to her son. "Ben, remind this lad to mind his elders. And his Elder. Now, heave ho and set sail."

"Aye, aye, captain," Jonathon said with a salute. "So, Samuel, Ben, are you joining our armada?"

"As long as Ben doesn't forget we're not on a submarine," Samuel quipped.

"Submarine?" Michael piped up. "Have you been on a submarine, Mr. Broader?"

"Yes. A long time ago. I served in the Navy."

"Cool! Will you tell me about it sometime, Mr. Broader?" Michael asked, his eyes wide.

"Sure, Michael, but only if you call me Ben."

Jonathon, Michael and Sarah put on life jackets and carefully climbed into the canoe. They paddled about twenty feet out and waited for Ben and Samuel to join them.

As they zipped up their life vests, Samuel asked, "Do you want front or back?"

"If you don't mind, I'll take the front," Ben answered.

"You trust me to steer?"

"Well, sort of. Mostly because the guy in the stern usually has to work a little harder. I'm just along for the ride."

Ben displayed spry balance getting into the front of the canoe. Samuel gave a push and stepped into the canoe—right on his neuroma. He winced and wobbled and almost tipped the boat before he was able to sit down and steady the vessel.

"Sorry about that, Ben."

"That would've made for a short voyage. You okay?"

"Just a mistimed step," Samuel said, unwilling to admit his right foot's poor condition. "Let's show that other boat that age and experience beats youth and arrogance every time," Samuel joked.

It didn't quite work out that way. Jonathon, Michael and Sarah were smooth as a team. Samuel struggled to keep up with them and Ben was content to idly paddle. At one point, Jonathon's canoe circled back and Sarah playfully splashed at Samuel.

"Is that all you've got?" she shouted.

"I think I'm more of a tugboat than a hydroplane," Samuel joked back.

He tried to splash her back, but only managed to get himself wetter. He gave up. Jonathon brought his canoe in closer.

"Michael wants to go up to the end of the lake. Are you guys up for it?"

Samuel looked behind him and saw they were just about in the middle. He was already feeling a bit winded. "No, I think we'll mosey on back. Take it leisurely."

"Okay. We'll be back in an hour or so," Jonathon said and waved as they started paddling up the lake.

Samuel waved back, wishing he had the energy to go with them. Then he turned back to find Ben frowning at him.

FACING FORWARD

WAS BEN REALLY SCOWLING AT HIM? THAT SEEMED out of character, so Samuel ventured, "Hope you didn't mind me making an executive decision about not going on, Ben?"

"Not at all," Ben said, his manner distracted. "You've been doing most of the paddling anyway."

"Well, I thought after all my swimming at the Y, I'd feel a bit stronger out here," Samuel confessed.

"Different muscles. Plus, I wasn't pulling my weight," Ben admitted. "I was thinking about tomorrow."

"I noticed you were a bit quieter than usual."

"Are you saying I'm chatty?" Ben asked with a more characteristic smile.

"Not chatty. You're witty. And you make some pretty astute observations." Samuel paused. "And speaking of observations, I don't think Fawn cares much for me."

Ben turned carefully in his seat to face Samuel. "What makes you say that?"

"She's been a bit aloof towards me."

"Have you made an effort to really talk to her?" Ben asked.

"I'm not real inclined to talk to people who don't seem so interested in being around me," Samuel responded. "I'd rather just go my own way."

"And that way leads to isolation. Samuel, do you think you're going to want fewer friends as you age?"

Samuel frowned. "I don't want fewer friends. I didn't want Thad to die. I can't control that."

"No, you can't. And Thad was a huge loss," Ben said. "But you *can* control whether or not you try to widen your circle of friends and acquaintances. In Eldering, we strive to network. It's one of the most important functions human beings have developed. We are social creatures. We depend upon one another. At any age, and particularly at our age, being in relationship with other people enhances our well-being and, thus, our survival."

"Are you saying that if I'm more of a loner, then I'm doomed?"

"Not necessarily, but the math and actuarial tables are not in your favor," answered Ben. "Remember, the key to what Eldering is all about is risk and renewal. Don't play it safe. Take chances. Do the things you've always wanted to try. Grow."

"How?"

"Turn towards people. Like I'm doing with you right now. When we began to talk, I physically turned towards you. But it's not just that. It also means you stay open to others. Take Fawn, for example. Just because you think she doesn't like you, don't turn away from her—turn towards her. Face her and reach out."

"What if she rejects that?" Samuel asked.

"Then that's her problem. You stay open to her. Don't shut anyone out, Samuel. It's an amazing way to let your circle of relationships grow. Leave doors open and you'll be amazed at who might walk through one day and say 'Hello.'"

"Might get a bit drafty with all those doors open," Samuel joked.

"Better a breeze or two than a stifling vacuum," Ben countered.

"I'm never going to win an argument with you, am I?"

"That's because you're afraid," Ben stated, matter of factly.

Samuel immediately became defensive. "Of what?"

"Of a lot of things. In this case, that you're wrong. That the way you've lived your life is wrong. That it's been a waste. No one at the end of a long life wants to admit that they lived their sixty, seventy, eighty years all wrong. Who wants to face that?"

Samuel sat silently for a few moments considering Ben's words. "So what do you do if you're faced with that possibility?"

"You row back to shore." Still facing Samuel in the canoe, Ben lifted his paddle. "Ready?"

As Samuel reached for his paddle, Ben started paddling. Samuel snorted, "We won't get very far if we're facing like this."

"Exactly my point, Samuel," Ben said, as he continued to paddle. "Until we're facing the same direction, paddling together, it's all wasted effort. So…which way will we follow? Whose way is right?"

Samuel watched Ben take long even strokes on either side of the canoe and asked, "If I dump the canoe trying to turn around in my seat, does that mean we should've taken my lead?"

"We'll never know until you make a move," Ben said with a poker face. "Sometimes you have to risk rocking the boat to see if your beliefs will sink or swim."

"Is that how you become an Elder?"

"Partly."

"What else does it take?" Samuel asked.

"Mostly courage to confront your fears and change despair into hope."

"Simple as that, eh?"

"Well, there's another little thing."

Samuel bit. "What's that?"

"You have to learn to die."

Samuel stared hard at Ben, who continued to paddle methodically. Slowly, Samuel shifted his weight and turned in his seat. The canoe wobbled slightly as Samuel inched his way around until he was facing away from Ben. He lifted his paddle and began to stroke with purpose, silently trying to decipher Ben's ominous words.

Live and Learn to Die

AS THEY CLOSED IN ON THE SHORE, SAMUEL turned back to Ben. "What did you mean about learning to die?"

Ben took a long pull with his paddle. "I suggest you learn that from the person who taught me."

"Fawn," Samuel guessed.

"She changed the course of my life—and Thad's," Ben explained. "She can be blunt and she can be inscrutable, but she is always honest."

"Brutally honest, maybe. And you don't think she's a curmudgeon?"

"She can be stubborn, but she's not a curmudgeon. She has hope and works to foster more hope. And she gets results." Ben lifted his paddle out of the water and set it across his knees as the canoe glided into the shallows. "You two might have more in common than you think."

Cheri stood up from her camp chair and waved. "How was it, boys?"

"Invigorating," Samuel yelled back as the canoe scraped bottom and slid to a stop. He gingerly stepped out of the boat and pulled it up onto the shore so Ben didn't have to get his boots wet.

As Ben climbed out, Samuel restated, "Yep, it was pretty nice out there."

"Well, good, but we don't want anyone wearing themselves out before tomorrow," Cheri reminded them with a wistful smile. "Speaking of which." She turned to Ben. "Can we talk about the ceremony?"

"Of course, Cheri. What would you like to know?" Ben asked.

Cheri stretched her arms into the air. "Do you mind taking a little walk, Ben? I've been reading the whole time you've been gone and I could use a short walkabout to get the blood circulating."

Ben smiled and nodded. "Certainly, my arms have just had a bit of a workout, so it'd be good to give my legs one too."

"Samuel, you're welcome to come too," Cheri invited.

"No, you two go on. I'm going to put my toes in the water. It'll do them good." Samuel, knowing the cold would soothe his neuroma, waved them on.

Cheri took Ben's arm and they headed up the trail that followed along the east side of the lake. Samuel sat down in a camp chair and took off his boots and socks. The lake water was frigid, yet refreshing. Samuel closed his eyes and let the warmth of the sunlight lull him into some peaceful shut-eye.

He awoke with a start. He felt a slight chill and a shiver, like a cloud had passed in front of the sun. He lifted his numb feet out of the water and shifted in his seat to set them down, dripping, onto his boots. That's when he noticed the figure in Cheri's chair.

Fawn.

Samuel was nonplussed. She must have slipped in from the trail while he'd dozed. She was sitting serenely, her eyes wide open, her hands cupped upward in her lap. She gazed upon the lake with love, as if it were her child.

He watched her, knowing she knew he was watching her. He turned his eyes, feeling the urge to slink away. He felt he would never measure up to her way of thinking, that he did not belong, that he was an intruder. Still, Ben had said she was a great teacher. What better challenge for her than a student like him?

Following Ben's suggestion, Samuel turned towards her. "Hi, Fawn. I didn't hear you come up. How was the hike?"

She did not turn to face him, but she answered, "Like coming Home."

She did not offer anything more, and Samuel felt he should say something else, but he remained still.

He was rewarded when Fawn began speaking of her own accord. "Our Mother will always welcome us if she remembers our footsteps. I walk in Her forests, so She will remember. So I will remember."

"That's a beautiful thought," Samuel said softly.

Fawn turned to him, her eyes still serene. "It's also a complete crock."

Samuel's jaw dropped. "What do you mean?"

"You're ready to buy anything I say because I'm an old squaw, right? You aren't trying to see me for who I really am—an educated, capable woman. You want to see me as some kind of mystical sage, an Indian shaman who can magically transform you by shaking some beads or blowing smoke in your direction. You're trying to typecast me like in some old Western."

"I was trying to be polite," Samuel growled.

"Try being real," Fawn replied in her even tone.

"According to you, I'm already a 'real' pain."

Fawn laughed a high short note. "Now you're talking! What's on your mind?"

Samuel looked at the stolid woman sitting off to his side in dismay. *What the heck was going on here?*

He risked a question. "Ben said you mentored both him and Thad. Why?"

"They didn't need me to hold their hands. They were seekers."

"Of what?" Samuel asked.

"Of themselves."

"Thanks for clearing that up," Samuel ventured sarcastically.

"You're welcome," Fawn replied evenly.

"Does this have anything to do with Ben telling me I needed to learn to die?" Samuel asked. "He said you taught him that."

"Actually," Fawn gave a cagey smile, "I lifted that from

Socrates. He said, 'We don't really have wisdom until we learn to die.'"

"So you get your best ideas from old dead white guys?"

"As long as they're old and dead."

"Ouch!" Samuel exclaimed. "Well, are you willing to clue in this old, barely living, white guy?"

She eyed him carefully. "Sure. As long as you're real. That's what I meant by Ben and Thad being seekers. They weren't pretending. They wanted to keep learning who they might become, what they might do. They weren't resigned to decrepitude. They weren't in denial about death or what they could do before their time ran out.

"They didn't fall prey to America's false gods of youth. What I call *wisdom*, the ability to help others be happy and fulfilled, is nurtured by living fully in the face of death. It means living in the present, focusing all one's being on what can be accomplished in this world now—not in the next. One has to forego immortality."

"There are a few religions that might challenge you on that," Samuel interjected.

"Wonderful," Fawn continued. "I believe in the spirit world. The older I get, the closer I get—the thinner the veil becomes. The mortality I'm speaking about is this bag of bones you see as Fawn. That's going to end."

"More cheery thoughts."

"Are your thoughts cheerier? I'm not at all afraid, but it appears that *fear and gloom* have become the focus of your whole life. I saw it the first time I looked into your eyes."

Samuel looked down at his glaringly white feet. "You

kind of wrote me off right then and there, didn't you? Samuel Block—not worthy."

"I *never* write anyone off. Ever," Fawn said with a conviction that made Samuel re-establish eye contact. "We are all sacred beings."

"Then are you going to help me?"

"Do what?"

"Learn to become an Elder like Thad or Ben," Samuel answered, feeling the need to understand.

Fawn looked back over Cooper Lake and said matter-of-factly, "That will never happen."

RIPPLE EFFECT

SAMUEL CLENCHED THE CAMP CHAIR TIGHTLY with both hands, feeling his face flush. "You just told me you never write anyone off."

"True. I don't. I have the patience of a redwood, but you will never be an Elder like Thad or Ben."

"Why not?"

"An Elder is the Self. You cannot be Thad or Ben or me. You have to trust yourself. To become *Samuel the Elder* you must be unafraid to be yourself. You must find the courage to face this last stage of your life and find a new purpose. Do you believe that is possible?"

"I don't know. Maybe with help. With guidance," Samuel muttered.

"Yes. You'll need guidance. That's why we have Eldering Circles. In many ways, the Circle reminds me of how our ancestors stored and shared their collective wisdom. Our young would seek knowledge and council from our elders. Each generation learning from the other. A cycle. A symbiosis. A sensible way to help and guide one another." Fawn paused and stood up. "But you'll need more than guidance."

Samuel's eyes semi-pleaded with Fawn. "Like what?"

"You'll need desire," she answered. "Not a curiosity. Not a cure. You have to feel drawn to a new purpose. To serve. It's not about what Eldering can do for you; it is about learning to share your talents, your experience and your wisdom with others. That is how to become an Elder."

Samuel let out a heavy sigh. "That's just the problem. I don't really think I have much to offer anymore. I guess, deep down, I don't think I matter much. I'm just another old guy, trying to eke out a few more years. I'm about as useful to myself and others as a pile of rocks."

Fawn watched him for a few moments, trying to decide something for herself. Then she reached down near the shore and picked up a couple of small stones. "Do you mean a pile of rocks for building a road or jetty or dam? Or do you mean a pile of rocks for creating the foundation of a great cathedral?"

In her hand, she turned the stones over and over in her palm and then held one out to Samuel. "How old do you think this stone is?"

"I'm no geologist. You're the one who's supposed to be close to Mother Nature. You tell me."

Undeterred by his sarcasm, Fawn said, "Well, take an educated guess."

"Thousands of years, maybe millions."

"That's pretty old. Older even than you. Let's see what it

can do." Fawn gripped the stone with her fingers and drew her hand back.

Samuel instinctively cringed. Fawn smirked. "Relax," she chided, "I'll give you fair warning if I intend to bean you for being closed-minded and full of self-pity." She turned and tossed the stone out into the lake where it landed with a reassuring *kerplop*.

She turned back to Samuel. "So what's that little old rock doing?"

"Sinking," he replied sardonically.

Fawn took another stone and drew her hand back. "Okay, I'm giving you fair warning. Any more of those Eeyore observations and it's right between the eyes."

Samuel comically raised his hands in front of his face as if to ward off any rock Fawn might heave at him. "Hey, you're the one who said I should be myself. We curmudgeons don't just burst out of our cocoons as optimistic butterflies. Give me some time."

"I'll give you two seconds. What did that little rock do?"

Samuel stood up and stared at the water. "Your little sinker is making ripples. I get the metaphor. Even little old me can make an impact and create some waves that become far-reaching."

"That's a start," Fawn acknowledged. "But let's extend the metaphor. That rock didn't jump off the shore and do that by itself. It needed help. It needed aim." She turned and tossed the second stone she'd been holding. It arced lazily along the shore until it fell almost silently into the tall grass at the water's edge. No ripples spread from its hidden impact.

114

"No aim. No purpose. Wasted effort. Got it?" she asked, turning back towards Samuel.

"Like water under the bridge," Samuel replied with a smile. "A big stone bridge."

"Good," Fawn remarked. "I hope the others return soon, so we can get back and start those ribs. Trying to feed you common sense makes me hungry."

STARTING A FIRE

EVERYONE WAS READY TO EAT BY THE TIME THEY got back to the cabin in the late afternoon. But there was neither microwave nor modern range. They had to cook the old-fashioned way: with fire. Out in the back of the cabin was a fire pit ringed by a wide stone patio.

Michael asked if he could help build the fire.

"Sure," Jonathon replied. "I have to get the ribs ready, but maybe Uncle Sam or Ben can help you."

"We'd be happy to help, young man," Ben said.

"Let's go split some kindling," Samuel said, motioning to the woodshed. He led Michael over to the lean-to that held split fir and hemlock. Samuel took out a few smaller pieces and handed Michael the hatchet. "Have you done this before?"

Michael handled the hatchet carefully, "Yes. My dad always watches me do it though."

"Okay," Samuel said, "Show me where you'd strike the wood."

Michael put a smaller split log on the stump next to the shed used for chopping. He placed the hatchet blade near the end of the cut log going along the grain. He looked back up at Samuel.

"That's right. Cutting with the grain is the way to go. Have at it."

Michael chopped while Samuel kept an eye on his hand position. In fifteen minutes, they had a nice pile of kindling. They gathered it up and carried it to the fire pit where Ben had balled up some newspapers.

Sarah and Fawn had come out to the back porch and set up a thick board between the two posts in the area the family used for food prep. They were chopping up peppers, mushrooms and onions and putting them in a grilling basket.

Sarah called over to the fire pit where Michael was carefully arranging the newspaper balls while Samuel and Ben watched. "Women prepping the food. The men playing with fire. Whatever happened to an equal division of labor?"

"*Playing* with fire! This is serious work. The 'quest for fire' is embedded deep in the male DNA," Samuel joked.

"Well, as long as it results in the 'quest for food' my appetite is seeking," Sarah shot back.

They all laughed. Even Fawn.

Michael had arranged the newspaper and was looking up at Samuel and Ben. "Teepee or cabin?"

Michael was asking about the arrangement of the kindling: should he stack it vertically leaning in on itself like a teepee or lay the sticks horizontally to form a log cabin.

"I'll defer to Ben on that," Samuel said.

"That's right," Michael chirped. "You were in the army. How'd they teach you to build a fire?"

Ben smiled kindly, "I was in the Navy and on a submarine, so we didn't build too many fires, but I've always been partial to the cabin method. I think it has to do with playing with Lincoln Logs as a child."

Michael's eyes grew wide. "I had Lincoln Logs. You mean they had Lincoln Logs when you were a kid?"

"Oh, yes. Very popular. I think they came right after the invention of the ball," Ben joked.

Michael smiled shyly, sensing that he had said something very young. He quickly built the cabin of kindling and stepped out of the fire pit. "I'll go get some matches," he said and started towards the back door of the cabin.

"Hold on," Fawn said, putting down the knife and wiping her hands on a towel. She stepped out from behind the cutting table. "Have you ever used a flint, Michael?" She pulled a small metal box from the pocket of her jeans and walked over to the fire pit, waving Michael over.

She demonstrated how to strike the small steel plate against the stone to generate a spark and then handed it to him. Michael mimicked Fawn's movements and was soon throwing small sparks into the pit. "Now, get the flint close to the newspaper," Fawn directed.

Samuel saw Sarah go into the cabin and within moments return with Jonathon and Cheri. Everyone watched as Michael struck the flint, scattering sparks onto the newspaper, some bouncing off the crumpled edges and some burning into the page.

A wisp of smoke rose from the paper. "Blow gently on it, Michael," Fawn directed.

Michael did and the edges where a spark had burned through glowed orange. He blew gently again and a small flame rose and started to creep outward. The flame quickly spread, reaching the kindling which crackled and popped as soon as the fire found the dry, crisp fuel.

Everyone clapped and Michael turned to see his dad and grandma and everyone watching. He smiled proudly. "Thanks," he said to Fawn, handing her the flint box.

Fawn patted his hand. "You keep it, Michael. I have another one."

Michael looked at his father, who nodded his approval.

"Thank you," Michael said. "I'll take good care of it."

"I'm sure you will, Michael. And pass it on when you're ready. You'll make someone else happy you've shared your knowledge," Fawn said.

Michael nodded and went to his father to show him. Folks started going back to their dinner-making duties. Samuel turned to go back to the woodshed for some larger pieces of the split wood to place on the fire. Ben joined him there.

"Did you see what just happened there?" Ben asked.

"Yeah, that was really kind of Fawn," Samuel acknowledged.

"It wasn't just Fawn. It was all of us. You helping Michael cut the kindling. All of us watchful and supportive. That was Eldering at its best. Adults with experience passing it on in very simple acts and in everyday conversations. Spontaneously. The willingness to help. I can't say what being an Elder means any better than what you just saw."

Samuel met Ben's eyes, burning bright with enthusiasm for what they'd just experienced, and, in that moment, Samuel felt a spark of understanding land somewhere in his soul.

As he carried an armful of logs back to the fire pit, he wondered if *that* spark would catch fire.

FIRE FOX

THE DINNER WAS FABULOUS. WHEN OUT IN THE forest by a fire, with the roar and tumble of a river nearby, tired out from canoeing, on a perfect spring day, even trail mix and ramen would make for a great dinner. But tonight they had a hearty feast: barbecued spare ribs Jonathon had cooked to perfection, grilled vegetables and a heavenly round of Cheri's homemade sourdough bread. The perfect way to scoop up excess barbecue sauce from the ribs.

They'd eaten out on the front porch with the evening sun casting a warm glow on the banks of the river, while they chatted and listened to the plan for the hike up Sahalie the next day. Cheri figured it would take them about four hours up and three hours back, so they decided to shoot for a nine o'clock start. They'd head out with a light lunch for the summit, hold the Eldering Ceremony and plan on being back to the cabin by six. Jonathon, Sarah and Samuel all agreed that the time frame sounded reasonable in light of all their ages. They'd all done that hike in a much shorter time before—but they'd all been much younger.

After clean up, daylight began to fade and Michael, who seemed to be waiting expectantly, asked, "Can we make S'mores?"

"Do owls hoot?" Sarah responded grabbing Michael's hand and heading towards the kitchen in the cabin.

As the air began to chill, the others grabbed camp chairs and headed around the cabin to the fire pit where embers glowed invitingly. Samuel went to the woodshed for a few more logs. As he brought them over and prepared to put one on the bed of orange coals, Cheri stopped him. "Samuel, you obviously haven't done this in a while. We want heat—not flames—to roast those marshmallows. You can build up the fire after that."

"Aww, I like the challenge of an open flame," Samuel playfully contested.

"Well, then you'll have to wait on your S'mores, young man," she chided in a most motherly fashion.

Luckily, no one had to wait. Sarah and Michael brought out the graham crackers, chocolate bars, marshmallows and several straightened wire coat hangers that had been well used. The feast became a competition to see who could get the most finely and evenly browned marshmallow. Sarah took that honor. "It must be the home court advantage," she laughed.

After their collective sweet cravings were sated, Samuel built up the fire and they enjoyed the added warmth and the primordial sense of security that the crackling flames provided under the darkening skies and forest around them.

Michael poked at some of the embers with his marsh-mallow-roasting coat hanger. "Does anyone have a good camp story?" he asked.

"You mean a ghost story?" Sarah asked back.

"No. Just a good story. I mean there's no TV and Dad won't let me bring my iPod."

"You bet he won't," Cheri said. "You're Grandpa wouldn't let you either. Right, Jonathon, Sarah?"

"Yup. That's always been the rule at Sahalie. No elec-tronics—except flashlights," Jonathon said and clicked on and off the one he had placed in the cup holder of his camp chair. "And that's just so we don't burn the place down at night relying on candles or oil lamps."

"That's why we need a story before you start talking about grown-up things," Michael pleaded.

"Like what?" his father asked curiously.

"News. Politics. Money. Doctors. That kind of stuff."

"Doctors?"

"Yeah, adults are always talking about medical stuff and who's got what disease."

"Guilty," said Sarah. "You know how old you are by how much you talk about what's going wrong in the health department."

"All right, Michael," his dad said. "We'll have a story, but then you better hit the hay. We've got a big day ahead of us tomorrow. Anyone have a story for our media-starved boy here?"

Fawn rose and stepped closer to the fire. Her face glowed dramatically against the dark sky above. "I have one—if you'd like to hear it," she said.

"Yeah, yeah," Michael whispered.

Surrounded by the golden light of the fire, Fawn began speaking in a rich, practiced voice:

When the land was much newer, a young fox came to live at the base of a tree that had long since died. Often an old owl would perch high above on the broken limbs of the tree. Sometimes the two would talk, though Owl was wary of Fox because he knew Fox was crafty and would try to eat him if given the chance.

One day, Fox was foraging in the forest and smelled something strange. His nose led him to look up and he saw a column of darkness rising over the hill where his home was. Even though he was a clever creature, he was puzzled because he had never seen such a dark cloud as this. He went back to his home and saw that Owl was watching the strange sight.

"Owl, old friend, what is that darkness rising over our hill?"

"Fox, my foe, that is smoke."

"Smoke? What is Smoke?" Fox asked.

"Smoke is a terrible creature that will choke you and kill you."

Fox was afraid. "Should we flee?"

"Not from that Smoke. It is the Smoke of the People." Owl explained.

"The People!" Fox gasped.

"Yes, I have seen them arrive. They bring their own trees

124

and make their own homes and will begin to hunt in our lands."

"And they will use Smoke to hunt us?" Fox asked appalled.

"No," Owl snorted. "The People have Smoke because they have a stronger power called Fire. They make Fire and Fire makes Smoke. Only the People and the Thunder Spear can make Fire. They use it for their own strange ways—not to hunt."

Fox became curious, "Why can we not make Fire? You are wise and I am clever. Why can we not have this power?"

Owl looked out over the hill towards the column of Smoke. "It is because I am wise that I do not try to make Fire."

But Fox only thought of what he would do if he could have the powers of Fire and Smoke. He raced over the hill and then stealthily approached the place where the People had come and made their People Trees. Fox crouched in the underbrush and watched the People.

Each day he came back to the same place and with his keen eyes studied the People. In this way, he learned how they made Fire. They gathered moss, twigs and branches from the forest. They placed the twigs upon the moss and then scratched one paw against a dark stone in their other paw. Bright sun specks flew from the stone onto the moss and the People would breathe upon it. Fire awoke and then Smoke rose.

Fox knew he could do this. He went back near his tree and began to collect all these things: moss, twigs and branches. He piled them near his home and then went to search for the dark stone. He found many dark stones and wore his claws *down scratching at them to make the sun specks fly, but he had no luck.*

At night, as Owl perched above, scanning the dark forest for his next meal, Fox dreamed of what he would do with Fire. He would become as powerful as the People. Fox would rule the land. So each day he gathered more and more moss, twigs and branches as he searched for the striking stone. Soon he had a huge pile gathered all around his tree. But without a stone like the People possessed, he did not have the power of Fire.

Desperate, Fox hatched a plan. If he could not find such a stone, he would steal one from the People. Being a crafty creature, Fox watched and waited until he saw his opportunity. One day, a small member of the People made Fire and set his striking stone down at his side. And then he disappeared inside a People Tree.

Fox did not hesitate. He dashed to the stone, snatched it in his jaws and sped back across the hill. At his tree, Fox dropped the stone and capered in delight. He would soon make Fire and then all the world would fear him.

His eyes darted to the top of the tree in search of Owl. He wanted to brag to him and say, "Who is wise now, old friend?" But Owl was not there, and Fox could not wait.

Moving towards the large pile of moss he'd gathered, he awkwardly clasped the striking stone in one of his paws. He raked his claws over the stone. It pained him, but he began to see tiny sun specks flying from his claws. He clawed faster and suddenly he saw a small Fire awaken in the moss. Fox moved close and breathed on it as he had seen the People do.

The Fire grew and Smoke filled Fox's nose. Fox sprang back from the Fire and the Smoke. Owl had been right. Fire and its evil-smelling Smoke could choke and kill. Fox moved cautiously backward as the Fire he had created grew and grew against his tree. Soon a dark column of Smoke that rivaled anything Fox had seen the People create surrounded his home.

This was the beginning. With this kind of power Fox would become king and all would bow before him. He basked in the warmth of his supremacy until a spark from the Fire leapt onto his coat. Fox yelped and then saw that the Fire was burning up his home and everything around it. He ran up the hill with Fire and Smoke in hot pursuit.

The next day, a weary and scorch-pawed Fox returned to his tree. All was ashes. The entire hillside had burned. He would have to find a new home, new hunting grounds.

Owl called to him from the very top of the only tree that had not been charred by the flames. "What have you learned about Fire, old foe?"

Fox looked around him at the blackened earth. He thought about his dreams of ruling all the land with this power. He thought about Pride and Greed and Foolishness. He considered Humility and Generosity and Wisdom. He glanced up at Owl who stared back like a thousand owls before him.

"Start small," Fox answered, a crafty gleam coming back in his eyes as he trotted off on a new path.

A Step Back

FAWN GAVE A SLIGHT BOW AS THE GROUP applauded loudly.

"Wonderful—though a bit morally ambiguous," Sarah exclaimed. "I like that."

"Fox sounds like a well-seasoned politician," Jonathon remarked.

Michael sighed. "See, Dad, you're starting to talk about politics. I'm going to bed."

"Not until you thank Fawn for her story," Jonathon coached.

"Thank you, Ms. Well. I liked your story."

"You're welcome. Everyone has stories to tell. Old and young. That's what the universe is really made of—our stories." Fawn smiled playfully at Michael. "Just don't get any ideas with that flint box I gave you earlier."

"No. I wouldn't want to burn down this place. It's too, too…," Michael paused and finished with a whisper, "…special."

Jonathon rose and put an arm around Michael's shoulder. Switching on his flashlight, he led his son towards the cabin and in through the back screen door. It closed behind them with a crisp slap.

Sarah turned to Cheri. "How's Michael doing?"

Cheri stared into the fire. "Oh, he's like all of us. He has his down times. You could ask the same question of each of us and it'd be the same. We miss Thad. Something—a place, a smell, a phrase he was fond of, the type of clothes he used to wear, a program he always watched, music he listened to...." She dabbed at her eyes with her sleeve. "Just takes a little to trigger a memory. But they're good memories. We're lucky that way."

Sarah scooted her chair closer and took Cheri's hand. "We are lucky. We had Thad for a long time. We'll always have him, and he gave us each other."

"It's a great gift to share one's friendships," Ben said. "Thad was able to do that so effortlessly."

Taking a seat, Fawn nodded solemnly. "It was Thad's fire. It blazed in him and he warmed other souls with it. He was Fox and Owl together."

"Yes, he was," Cheri sighed, "and tomorrow we'll spread the ashes of his last fire."

"No, Cheri," Fawn said with great warmth. "Thad's sense of purpose continues to smolder in us. The right breath, the right breeze will make it blaze in unexpected places, just like those memories of him." She looked carefully around at each of them, stopping on Samuel. "One never knows where his fire, his passion to live life fully, will catch."

129

Samuel could not meet Fawn's eyes. He looked across at Sarah, whose eyes danced in the firelight. She smiled at him, and he relaxed as if she'd given him another hand massage.

As if by mutual agreement, the five sat in silence. Samuel followed several sparks from the fire as they floated upward and melted into the darkness. *Did he have Thad's spark? His passion for life?* His gaze continued upward to the stars coming out. Small pinpoints that represented huge suns. Worlds upon worlds. Samuel thought about his world. *What was really important? What did he have to offer?*

The stars seemed to blur together and spin. Feeling a bit dizzy, he closed his eyes, rubbing them with his fists.

"Tired?" Ben asked.

"Yeah, it's been a long day. I think I'll turn in," Samuel said, looking forward to snuggling up in his sleeping bag on the upstairs porch and being alone with his thoughts.

Sarah and Cheri stood up as well. "Yeah, me too," Sarah said. "It always takes a bit longer to get ready for sleep up here with no running water."

"You've got plenty of running water. Just listen," Samuel motioned towards the front of the cabin.

"That's more like *sprinting* water. It wouldn't leave a lick of toothpaste on my toothbrush. And not too easy to swallow those nightly pills drinking from the river either," Sarah teased back.

"Oh, right, meds before bed. Our new mantra," Samuel said.

Sarah and Cheri laughed. "See you in the morning,"

Cheri said, turning on a flashlight. Sarah followed her path of light into the cabin.

Samuel turned to Fawn and Ben. "Would you like me to put out the fire?"

"No," Fawn said. "Ben and I are staying up to talk about the ceremony tomorrow. We'll let it die out before we come in."

"Goodnight, then," Samuel said and started around the side of the cabin. He intended to go sit on the front porch and listen to the river for a while to decompress. Ben and Fawn had given him a lot to think about, and he needed the time to collect his thoughts.

In the enveloping darkness away from the fire pit, Samuel fumbled in his fleece jacket for his flashlight. He pulled it out and clicked the button. Nothing. He shook the flashlight and tried again. It still didn't work. *Figures,* he thought with a grim smile. *Just another equipment failure in my life.*

He could make out the vague outline of the cabin to his left, so he slowly moved forward with his hands outstretched. When his fingers contacted the weather-polished logs of the cabin he used it as a guide and carefully made his way to the edge of the porch.

Samuel was stepping up onto the porch when his foot caught a stone and he lurched forward. The ball of his right foot came down hard on the edge of the step.

Pain seared up from his foot through his entire leg.

He limped onto the porch and found one of the Adirondack chairs with his outstretched hands and slumped into it. The roar of the river mixed with the burning pain in his foot. Breathing deeply, he fought to control the pain. It always seemed to come back to that fight for control: what he wanted to do and what his body let him.

Both Fawn and Ben had tried to tell him not to focus on the aches and pains of aging, that Eldering was about keeping one's personal fire lit—the flame to aspire to inspire others. They made it sound so easy. As if the desire alone was enough.

But for Samuel, the only fire he felt at the moment was his blazing neuroma. A familiar sense of dread and foreboding crept into his thoughts. It was going to be a long, painful day tomorrow. Sitting there, dealing with his hobbled foot, he felt defeated, like he'd already let Thad, his family and himself down.

ASCENDING

EVERY STEP BURNED. THEY WERE ONLY A HALF mile along the trail and already Samuel felt he was reaching his threshold of endurance. Tripping onto the porch last night had really done it. He'd hardly slept at all with the radiating pain and the fear he'd start groaning and awaken Fawn on the other side of the sleeping porch. Buried deep in his sleeping bag, he'd bit his lip and endured the pain, panic, anger and frustration of his situation.

Putting on his right boot that morning had been agonizing. He'd popped four ibuprofen first thing, which helped him get through breakfast and the preparations for the hike up to Sahalie. Unable to hide his slight limp, Jonathon had asked him if he was okay. Samuel had tried to downplay his concern, saying it was just his old bones protesting the early start. He couldn't let anyone think he wasn't up to this. He had to do it for Thad. For himself.

Now, with the ibuprofen having mostly worn off, the pain was growing in intensity. He'd lagged behind, so that he was bringing up the rear. He didn't want anyone to know. At the moment, the trail was rather tame. They were winding through a light stand of second growth Douglas firs filled with huckleberry bushes. Samuel remembered how he and Thad had feasted on huckleberries here one July. At the moment, he wished they were painkiller bushes and he could pick a few little red pills.

He had more ibuprofen in his daypack, but he didn't want to stop. He knew they'd notice if he lagged any further behind. Especially Fawn. She seemed to be watching him more closely. Waiting for something.

Well, Samuel wasn't going to be the one anyone waited on. This was grind time on a grand scale. He was going to take it one painful step at a time until he got to the top. He concentrated on the trail, trying to place each footstep as carefully as he could.

Up ahead, he heard Michael talking to Ben about being on a submarine during WWII. Ben patiently answered all his questions, taking extra care to focus on the humor and the positive aspects of his experiences. Samuel remembered how Ben had confided in him over a cup of coffee at *A Hill of Beans* about being exposed to the horror of battle and the injustices of war as a young man.

Ben seemed to know what people needed. He was telling Michael the truth about his service in the Navy, but at the same time protecting him from the cruelties of war. He was keeping Michael safe, while helping him grow. A sense of admiration for Ben took root in Samuel, and he speeded up a bit to stay more connected to the group.

After the grove of huckleberries, the trail steepened and the group bunched closer together. Samuel caught up to Cheri and Sarah who were a few paces behind Ben and Michael. Jonathon led the way about 20 feet in front of them, with Fawn a few steps behind.

"How are you doing?" Samuel asked, masking his discomfort with a smile.

"Just taking it slow," Sarah answered.

"Enjoying the memories," Cheri said. "I haven't been up to Sahalie in years. I'll never forget the first time Thad brought me up here. It was in mid-August, a few months after we'd begun dating. We climbed up late in the afternoon, so we could have a light dinner at the top and watch the sunset. As the sky turned red, Thad told me how much it meant to him that I'd been willing to make the climb."

Sarah giggled. "I'll bet. One summer in our teens, Thad and I climbed Sahalie. We were sitting up there having a snack, and he told me he didn't think he could really fall in love with someone who didn't love Sahalie." Sarah sighed. "I guess I should've taken his advice and made my first two husbands climb it before I married them."

Cheri stopped and gave Sarah a hug. "As much as that sunset on Sahalie was one of the most romantic moments of my life, it was also one of the scariest. Thad and I stayed to enjoy the glorious sunset and ended up leaving later than we should have. We had to hustle down that narrow ledge near the top with the light starting to fade."

Sarah's eyes grew wide. "Yeah. That part of the trail is ridiculous when it's getting dark," Sarah remarked.

"It can be plenty scary—even in broad daylight. That tight ledge next to a 300-foot sheer drop still gives me the willies." Cheri paused. "Jonathon told me that he's concerned about what Michael will do when he sees that part of the trail."

"Is he afraid of heights?" Samuel asked, envisioning the ledge near the peak of Sahalie they were discussing.

"Not an out-and-out fear, but he avoids high exposed places," Cheri explained. "Jonathon knows it may be tough for him, but he also knows how much this means to Michael."

"Yeah," Samuel said. "I was impressed that he wanted to carry the urn."

Cheri nodded. "He's been talking about it for weeks, so I think he'll be fine."

"We'll all be there to help him," Sarah said.

The conversation stopped as they maneuvered through a tight series of switchbacks that brought them above a stand of trees and onto a meadowy slope. Down below they could see the river winding through the forest. They had gained about 500 feet in elevation. Another 1,000 to go. *Grind it out, Block,* he told himself.

He did. Scrambling over trees that had fallen over the trail. Up another steep series of switchbacks. And then, when his pain had become almost unmanageable, they stopped for a break. It was a place Samuel remembered well. It was the halfway point to the top where the trail wound its way through large formations of rock creating a series of broad shelves above the Salmon la Sac River.

One of the larger formations actually cantilevered over the river. It was here that Thad and Samuel had once tied themselves off to a nearby boulder and leaned out over the abyss. Three hundred feet of empty space to the raging river below.

Wanting to be alone, Samuel moved out on to the broad rock that hung over the river. He plopped down and rummaged in his daypack. He retrieved four ibuprofen and gulped them down with a long drink from his water bottle.

A shadow fell across him. "You sharing?" Sarah asked, eyeing the pill container.

"At our age, I thought this was BYOM," Samuel joked.

Sarah shot him a give-me-the-punch line look.

"Bring Your Own Meds."

"Well, I did. I just happened to leave them at the cabin, and I'm going to have one sore knee if I don't try to keep the swelling down."

Samuel handed her the bottle. "Thanks," she said. "What's ailing you? I can see you're trying to hide your limp. Is it anything serious?"

Samuel hadn't wanted to tell anyone about his neuroma, thinking it would make him seem weak. Like he was old. But wasn't he old? What did he have to fear by admitting the truth? Fawn had told him to be real. And if there was anyone he wanted to be real with, it was—he suddenly realized—Sarah.

"Honestly? I've got a nasty neuroma on my right foot. I stepped on it wrong going to bed last night, and it's killing me."

"Ouch," she sympathized. "You willing to let me try something?"

"Like throwing me off that cliff?" he motioned behind them.

"Not quite that radical. Remember the hand massage I gave you yesterday?"

"Hard to forget that," Samuel said with a silly grin.

"Okay, I'm going to try some pressure points on your neck and face. I don't know if it'll do any good, but hopefully it may help a little," Sarah explained.

"I'm game," Samuel said.

"Alright, try to relax." She moved behind him and began a series of pressure and release holds on his temples, jaw, and upper and lower neck.

The whole process took about two minutes. "Is that any better?" Sarah asked as she took a seat across from Samuel.

Samuel wiggled the toes of his right foot. "Definitely," he said. It did feel better. The neuroma hadn't magically disappeared, but the piercing pain was gone. He just felt soreness. A very manageable soreness.

"Thanks," he said. "I wish you could bottle those hands. I'd trade in my ibuprofen for them."

Sarah blushed a bit. "I'm just a hack. The pros really know what they're doing."

"Well, so do you. With a skill like that, you'd be everybody's favorite Elder."

"Elder?" Sarah smiled quizzically. "Honestly, I still don't know what that really means." She paused a moment, sighed and turned to look out across the valley below. "And it's a bit strange since we're going to make Thad a posthumous Elder in just a couple of hours."

Samuel nodded. "I feel the same way. Ben and Fawn have made my head spin with some of their ideas." He motioned back towards the trail where Fawn and Ben sat on a log. "They seem to be certain that Eldering is the answer. And you have to admit, they're impressive people."

"True," Sarah said. "I don't think I'm quite their caliber. They've had such fascinating lives."

"I know what you mean, Sarah. Honestly, I've wanted to find a reason to dismiss this whole Eldering thing as just a way for old people to feel good about themselves," Samuel admitted. "But when I see how confident they are, when I see how sure about the future they seem, I get the feeling they understand something I don't."

"Yes. Plus the fact that Thad got so involved. You know he wasn't someone to climb on just any old bandwagon."

"Right," Samuel agreed. "Thad was very much his own thinker."

They fell silent as Jonathon approached. "Hey, you two are kind of living on the edge over here." He walked just past them to within three feet of the canyon and looked over the drop-off. "Pretty expansive view from here."

He turned back to where Sarah and Samuel sat. "I tried to get Michael to come over and look at the view of the river, but no go," he said in a lowered voice. "I even tried to coax him over by letting him know that right below us is the infamous Ron's Canyon. I thought it would be a good gauge of how he'll do on the ledge."

"You think he'll be able to handle that last stretch before the top?" Sarah asked with concern.

"I don't know. I remember when Dad first took me up there. I was pretty scared and heights don't really bother me. I know how badly Michael wants to make it, but I don't want to push him into something he can't do." Jonathon let out a deep breath.

"Don't worry, we'll keep him safe," said Samuel.

Samuel was as surprised as Sarah and Jonathon that he'd been the one to open his mouth and make that promise.

Parallel Paths

SAMUEL DIDN'T HAVE MUCH TO WORRY ABOUT with Michael as they started up the second half of the trail. From the cliffs above Ron's Canyon, the trail turned away from the Salmon la Sac River and headed into the mountains. The trail climbed steadily upwards. At times, they had to scramble up steep sections using smaller trees and their branches as a kind of handrail, but Michael, sharing the point with his father, seemed at ease and even enthusiastic.

Samuel, too, was more enthusiastic. Because of the ibuprofen and Sarah's pressure point therapy, the pain of his neuroma had subsided. As they gained elevation, he felt better able to appreciate the sun dappling through the thinning forest. He also enjoyed Sarah's company. She had joined him at the back of the pack and they talked when the trail wasn't too strenuous.

Samuel found her very easy to talk to. She got him telling stories about his grandson, Jimmy, and even about

Rolf, his stoic swimming buddy at the YMCA. He realized it had been a long time since he'd chatted so freely with anyone—let alone with a woman.

At one point, Sarah began sharing more memories of Thad and her at the cabin when they were young. "Being at Sahalie, I could never really picture what the future would be like. I always thought I'd be the same whenever I came here."

"This place does make me feel younger," Samuel agreed, "though my body keeps telling me otherwise."

"Yes. The clock keeps ticking, but I never thought about growing older like my parents—or grandparents. I remember my grandparents seeming so old when I was a kid, and they were probably only fifty or so."

"I know what you mean. I think we Baby Boomers never expected to grow shuffleboard old like that. Like if we kept dressing young, driving sports cars and listening to The Beatles and the Stones we wouldn't end up in nursing homes. Doesn't quite work that way, I guess," Samuel reflected.

"Yeah, but keeping active and staying positive sure helps."

"It's that staying positive part that's hard for me," Samuel admitted.

"Even with Jimmy? He sounds like he's the light of your life," Sarah asked.

"Well, he is," Samuel beamed. "But you know, work, making ends meet, dealing with health issues. They seem to weigh me down."

"Do you get out much?" Sarah asked.

"Well, for work I do. But I keep pretty much to myself in the evenings—though I did push myself to swim and work out to be ready for this hike."

"Did that help?"

"Yeah," Samuel said. "But now that I've almost reached my goal of making it up Sahalie with all of you, I worry that I'll fall back into my old habits."

"Well, I hope it doesn't make you a complete stranger. I...," she hesitated, "Cheri and I wouldn't want to lose touch." Sarah turned her flushing face back to the trail.

Samuel smiled to himself, concentrating on Sarah's last words as they moved cautiously along a seemingly new path in their lives. A path that paralleled the dirt and rock trail leading them steeply up to Sahalie's peak.

TO THE EDGE

ABOUT THIRTY MINUTES LATER JONATHON stopped up ahead and both Samuel and Sarah knew why. They were just a quarter mile from the top of Sahalie and the trail was about to take a sharp turn. The last of the thinning trees would be behind them and they would have an unobstructed view of the river basin and the breath-taking peaks of the central Cascades.

But it was the view of the trail just around the bend that Samuel feared might just take the breath away from Michael. The trail arced around a massive granite outcropping that formed the crown of Sahalie. For thirty yards, the trail followed a two-foot-wide ledge that was solid and provided good footing, but was completely exposed on the west side. A sheer drop.

Samuel remembered that, even though he had been an experienced hiker the first time he'd climbed up here with Thad, he'd still felt a moment or two of vertigo on this exposed portion of the trail. He worried how Michael might react when he saw the ledge up ahead.

Jonathon was speaking quietly to Michael at the side of the trail. The rest of the adults huddled together.

"Jonathon's trying to prepare Michael," Cheri told them. "He thinks he'll be motivated enough to give it a try."

"But we need to have a plan if he freezes or panics on the ledge," Sarah advised.

Samuel nodded. "If Michael doesn't think he can do it, I'll stay here with him, and the rest of you go on." Sensing polite objections, Samuel continued. "Ben and Fawn need to do the Eldering Ceremony. You all are Thad's family. It just makes the most sense to me."

"Okay," Cheri agreed. "That does make sense, but let's hope it doesn't come to that."

Cheri went over to Jonathon and Michael. She sent Michael over to the other adults while she and Jonathon spoke.

Michael looked a bit downcast when he came and stood next to Sarah.

"Hey, chin up, Michael," Sarah said. "You'll be fine."

"I'm gonna do it," Michael said, as he bit down lightly on his lip.

"We'll get you up there," Ben encouraged.

Cheri and Jonathon joined them. Jonathon put on a show of supreme optimism. "Twenty minutes and we're at the top. Everyone ready?"

"Yes," Michael answered for them.

"Excellent. So, this is the plan. Samuel's going to lead,

then Michael, then me. The three of us will follow the ledge first and we'll wave you over when we get to the spot where the trail widens again. That sound okay?" Jonathon asked.

"Yes," Michael answered again, and tightened the belt strap on his pack containing the urn that held his grandfather's ashes. A confidence showed in his features that belied his tender age.

Samuel patted Michael's shoulder and took the lead. Michael and his father fell in behind. They marched around the bend and the whole river basin opened up before them. The mighty peaks of Adams and Rainier floated above a carpet of green. Saw-toothed mountain ranges fanned out like waves, frothing with their caps of snow and ice. It was spectacular, and Samuel glanced back to see how Michael was taking it in.

Not well, he could see. He'd slowed and his father's hands were on his shoulder. Michael was still moving forward, but only reluctantly. The trail quickly narrowed and to their left the mountainside fell away. They were at the ledge.

Samuel felt it best to just keep moving. He slowed his pace so that Michael and Jonathon were able to come up close behind. "We'll just take it slow now," Samuel said to them. "Feel free to hold onto my backpack, if that helps, Michael."

Jonathon added, "And, Michael, I'll be holding onto your backpack. We're a team. Okay?"

Samuel felt a tug on his backpack straps and knew that Michael had grabbed hold. He took a couple of small steps onto the ledge, then turned his head to check on Michael.

The boy had locked his eyes on Samuel's backpack. That was good. It would help him stay focused and avoid the temptation to look over the side.

Samuel kept the pace at a crawl, and they slowly marched a third of the way without any problem. Then, a few feet ahead, Samuel noticed a rock about the size of his fist sitting in the middle of the path. To prevent anyone stumbling on it, Samuel kicked it out of the way. It tumbled noisily over the side.

Immediately, he felt his pack tugged backwards. He glanced back at Michael. The young man's eyes were focused on the seemingly depthless void into which the rock had disappeared.

Michael froze. His hands were clenched so tightly on the backpack that Samuel could not turn for fear of knocking the boy off balance.

Jonathon recognized what was happening and spoke softly to his son, "It's okay, Michael. Uncle Sam was just clearing the path for us. That's why I wanted him to lead. He's done this before. Many times—with your grandpa."

Michael did not answer. His eyes were fixated on the drop off to their left. Samuel felt his backpack shaking. Michael was starting to panic.

Samuel slowly slipped out of his pack, holding it tightly by the straps. He turned so he was facing Michael and Jonathon. Beyond them he could see Cheri, Sarah, Ben and Fawn looking on with concern. Sarah took a step out onto the ledge. He met her eyes and motioned "No" with his head. Sarah stepped back with a nod of understanding.

THE ELDER

Samuel stared at Michael, who remained focused on the void. Taking Jonathon's lead, speaking softly but clearly, he said, "Look at me, Michael. Your dad is right. Grandpa Thad and I have done this many times. He always made me feel safe. And he's still with us. You're carrying him."

Michael's eyes blinked.

"Good," Samuel encouraged, "Your dad and I are here. We're going to keep you safe. Now, take a deep breath."

Samuel's pack continued to shake. "A deep breath, Michael," Samuel patiently reminded.

Michael blinked again and his head turned back towards Samuel. "Deep breath," Samuel said and inhaled noisily.

Samuel made eye contact with Jonathon and breathed deeply again. Jonathon understood. "Deep breaths, Michael. Like Uncle Sam and I," he coached, inhaling noisily.

Jonathon and Samuel let out their breaths together. They inhaled and exhaled in unison a few times. Michael stayed focused on Samuel's exaggerated breathing. Then his eyes locked on Samuel's. His eyes pleaded.

Samuel had never felt such need before—not even in his own grandson, Jimmy. Michael's eyes were begging him to make the paralyzing fear go away. In that moment, Michael's entire being depended on Samuel and no one else.

The realization pushed Samuel off balance. A kind of emotional vertigo. The sheer demand of Michael's raw need stunned him. *Can I really help him? Do I have it in me?*

He was at the edge. Staring into the void, the unknown. His own indecision was threatening to swallow him, and

148

with him, Michael. Could he face this on his own? Without Thad to lead him?

Was there really a choice?

The question, a millisecond in the making, swept away his second-guessing. In this here and now, there was only one thing to do.

He met Michael's eyes. Held them carefully. He let Michael pour out his fear. His doubt. His primal need for help. Samuel's eyes took it all in and gave back—his certainty, his confidence, his commitment—with each deep, steady breath.

Gradually, the rhythm of Michael's breathing joined his and Jonathon's. The young boy's shaking diminished and his eyes gradually calmed.

Not breaking eye contact with Michael, Samuel asked. "Okay, Michael, do you want to turn around and go back?"

In a terse, hoarse whisper, Michael responded immediately, "No."

"Jonathon?" Samuel asked.

"I'm with Michael. All the way," Jonathon said softly, confidently. He gave Samuel a nod as if to say, *And you too.*

"Okay. You ready, Michael?"

Michael did not break eye contact. "Yes."

Samuel smiled. "Okay. Let's try something. I want you to turn so you're facing away from the cliff and put your hands against the side of the mountain."

Michael let go of Samuel's backpack one hand at a time and inched around so his back was to the void. Samuel slowly slipped his pack onto his shoulders so as not to draw attention.

"Now, Jonathon. Let's you and I grab each other's wrist and make like a rope around Michael's waist." They did.

"You feel that, Michael. Your dad and I are your safety line. You just move at your own pace with your feet and hands, and we'll move with you."

Nodding, Michael began to shuffle his feet along the ledge, with his hands against the mountainside. Gradually, he took bigger sideways steps.

"Doing great," Jonathon coached. "We're halfway across."

Keeping their wrists locked, Samuel and Jonathon moved slowly along with Michael. Five eternal minutes later, Samuel stepped from the two-foot-wide ledge to the much wider and more protected trail that wound tightly to the top of Sahalie. Michael and Jonathon followed a few feet up the trail where they released the protective grip on their wrists.

Jonathon grabbed his son in a bear hug. "You did it!" he said proudly.

Samuel looked back to the edge—where the ledge ended and the sheer, dizzying drop began. He was amazed at the void, the ominous emptiness they'd just crossed. In that moment, he felt that Jonathon's words to Michael could just as easily have been meant for him.

Making It Safe

SAMUEL MOVED BACK ONTO THE LEDGE TO GET a better line of sight with the others. He waved back to Cheri, Sarah, Ben and Fawn, indicating that they should come across. Then Samuel moved up the trail and sat down on a cluster of boulders about ten yards from the end of the ledge.

Jonathon and Michael joined him. "Well done, Michael," Samuel said, holding up a hand to high five.

Instead, Michael clasped his hand tight and said, "Thanks for helping me, Uncle Sam."

Samuel gave his hand a squeeze and looked him right in the eyes. "Any time. Always."

"You and Dad didn't give up on me."

"We wouldn't think of it."

"Someday," Michael said, still clutching Samuel's hand, "I hope I can learn to do what you did for me."

"You will. In a way, you just did," Samuel said giving Michael's hand a squeeze back.

Michael looked at Samuel quizzically, and then he was plucked away by his grandmother, the first of the others to make it across the ledge. Cheri squeezed him in her arms. "I'm so proud of you. Grandpa would be too." She led him off a few feet and fussed over her only grandson.

Jonathon took the opportunity to shake Samuel's hand. "Thanks, Sam. You got us both through that."

Samuel shook his head. "No. I didn't do anything. I just tried not to panic myself."

"I don't think I would've had the sense to keep going forward, which was the safest thing to do. I would've tried to turn him around. Force him back," Jonathon admitted in a low voice.

"Moving forward seemed like the right thing to do at the time, but it took both of us to make him feel secure," Samuel said. His words brought to mind his own son and grandson. Maybe they needed him in this way, too.

"Well, I'm just glad you were in the lead," Jonathon declared. "And I want you there on the way down."

Samuel nodded absently. He wasn't used to thinking of himself as the leader. That had always been Thad's role. For most of his life, Samuel had been a follower—and often a reluctant one.

One by one, Fawn, Ben and Sarah came across the ledge and assembled around them. Cheri returned to the group holding Michael's hand. She faced Jonathon and Samuel. "As much as I'm proud of Michael, I'm just as proud of both of you."

"Nothing to it," Jonathon downplayed. "Now, let's get to the top. Then we can celebrate with some lunch." He took Michael's free hand and started up the trail with his son and mother in tow.

Ben offered his hand to Samuel who took it and stood up. "Nicely done out there."

Samuel thought about Michael's eyes. His overwhelming need. "He was so scared." Samuel halted. "The unknown is terrifying. He just needed us to make him feel safe."

"Yes," Ben said quietly. "That's what Eldering is all about. Making it safe for people to take risks and grow."

A little embarrassed, Samuel looked away from Ben to see Fawn looking at him intently. She met Samuel's eyes and gave an approving nod. Samuel was surprised, and pleased. Then she turned and continued up the trail to join the group. Ben patted Samuel's shoulder. "Now you see why she doesn't do a lot of hand-holding. See you at the top," he said as he followed after Fawn.

Samuel wasn't sure if he was as ready to spread his wings into Eldering as Fawn had just hinted, but his spirit soared at her and Ben's acknowledgement. He didn't know how it could get any better.

Until.

Sarah stepped up to him. "I guess they're beginning to see what Thad always did—and what I'm starting to see in you." She lightly kissed him on the cheek and whispered, "Thanks for making me feel safer, too."

THE ELDER

AT THE TOP OF SAHALIE, THE GROUP SAT IN A
circle. The urn containing Thad's ashes rested in the middle.
The brilliant blue clarity of the mountain sky surrounded
them, and although the May sun shone warmly, a westerly
breeze kept them comfortably cool.

They'd had their lunch and meandered about the rocky
dome dotted with hardy patches of heather and a few small
patches of snow. For Samuel, being on Sahalie again, floating over the Salmon la Sac River Basin, he felt the presence
of Thad. They had been there together so many times. But
on this day, he'd made it to the top without his best friend,
despite his worries and his neuroma. And he'd been there
for Michael.

He'd kept a promise to himself and to Thad. He felt
more in charge of his life than he had in a long, long time.
And with Sarah there was an emotional connection he
hadn't experienced in years, and it made him realize he'd
discounted a lot of his relationships with others. Now he

was beginning to see how personally impoverished that had left him. He needed others and needed to be needed by others.

Like the famous adage taught: growing up—and growing old—really did take a village. And Samuel had to find his new place in it. When Ben called them all together to begin the ceremony, Samuel was feeling, for the first time, that he truly belonged with this group.

They formed a tight circle and Ben started, "Though Fawn and I will conduct the ceremony, it is all of you who will acknowledge Thad's life and how he contributed to others. To be an Elder is not about achieving a certain age: it's about embracing a wellspring of experience and sharing it with others.

"It's not too lofty or idealistic for Elders to believe they can change the world—one interaction at a time. It's our credo. An Elder focuses on the everyday opportunities to offer kindness, caring and assistance to everyone. Thad embraced that outlook and it is entirely fitting that he be remembered and honored as an Elder today."

Ben paused for a moment and then continued. "There are many facets to the Eldering Ceremony that Fawn and I will not include today, but we will do the most important part, which is the sharing. Each of us will share what Thad personally 'gave' to us."

He motioned to Fawn. "Fawn is an Elder's Elder. She has passed on her wisdom and understanding to me, to Thad and many others who have formed Eldering Circles. I've asked her to be the first to share her thoughts on Thad."

Fawn solemnly nodded. She closed her eyes and did not speak for a few moments. She held her arms wide and began. "In this place of my forefathers and mothers, my heart is open. To Thad. To all of you. That is the promise of Eldering. An opening of the arms to others and to life itself. A commitment to passing along a lifetime of understanding. Some mistakenly call that wisdom. But understanding is not wisdom. Being wise is about sharing our perspective with others in a way that helps them develop their own ability to choose well in the situations they encounter.

"In that, Thad became wise. Whereas many reach an age where they believe it is their time to reap the fruits of their labors and 'retire' from the march of the world, Thad did the opposite. He recommitted. He made the choice to re-engage with the world—one person at a time.

"Thad learned the secret of living his life for others. You have no fears for yourself when you live for others. You strive to help others take on the challenges they need in order to grow. That is the basis of the deepest compassion and the origin of the most selfless actions. In this way, Elders lead. In this way, Thad became and will always be an Elder. His example lives in each of us—and has the power to teach us all."

Samuel, struck by the grace and sincerity of Fawn's speech, noticed that she ended her last sentence looking directly at him. This time he didn't feel intimidated or unworthy. Although he sensed the challenge, he felt her gaze was like that of a coach who sees in a player the potential for success—and calls on them to commit to become the best they can be.

Ben thanked Fawn and asked who wanted to share next. Surprisingly, Michael spoke up. He talked about his grandpa's gift of time to him. Teaching him to fish, to ski and the time they built a catapult together for a school Science Fair.

Jonathon followed his son and spoke about his father's gifts of humor and optimism and how they had taught him to look for the positive and to learn to laugh at the absurdities of modern life.

Samuel, not wanting to go last, feeling that was Cheri's privilege, said very plainly that Thad's gifts to him were his love of the outdoors and the lessons learned during their decades of hiking. And how Thad's 'grind time' philosophy was something that was still enabling him to work through tough times.

There was much more Samuel wanted to say, but he could not yet convey the depths of his experience out on the ledge and immediately afterwards. Yet, on a fundamental level, something in him had changed. Something that Thad and everyone gathered here had had a part in. Samuel felt a new possibility, a new perspective growing in him. And this allowed him a sense of peace, of intense well-being, as he publicly acknowledged the great debt he owed to his best friend.

Ben followed with the story of how Thad had been skeptical about what Eldering was and could accomplish. Ben explained how Thad had challenged him to get to the core of his own beliefs in order to clearly articulate what Eldering meant. Thad had given the gift of clarity to Ben and strengthened the courage of his convictions.

Sarah, becoming teary-eyed, told how Thad always made her feel safe. That there was no more important gift anyone could provide, because it was almost impossible to take chances and grow and learn as a human if you didn't feel safe. She stressed that Thad didn't think that, as a woman and his sister, he needed to protect her from the dangers of the world. But he understood that everyone needed that trust that someone would be there to help them up if they stumbled or fell. When Sarah finished, there was a sustained silence, as if in acknowledgment of the very recent events out on the ledge.

Then Cheri spoke of gratitude. She told them all how Thad had taught her the gift of gratitude. To be grateful for each and every day. To show it often in simple words and actions. Thad had told her he believed gratitude was the real language of love, and Cheri confessed that she still thanked him aloud every day for their time together.

Luckily, Sarah had thought to put tissues in her backpack. It was one of those moments when tears felt like the only way to express the truth.

"Thank you, everyone," Ben said in wrapping up the ceremony. "Your heartfelt expressions of Thad's gifts are exactly what the Eldering Ceremony is intended to be. Thad is now an Elder and will be so designated in the Bainbridge Island Elder Circle."

They all applauded. Jonathon then rose. "Michael,

come over and help me," he called. The two moved to the urn and Michael lifted it. "Cheri and I would like each of you to help spread my father's ashes. Everyone here was very important to him."

Michael took the lid off the urn. Sarah rose first and moved closer to them, holding out her palm. Jonathon helped Michael gingerly pour some of Thad's ashes into her cupped hand. She covered her brother's ashes with her other hand.

One by one, the rest of the group stepped up. When they all had their hands cupped together, cradling the last piece of Thad they would ever touch, Cheri turned to Fawn. "Fawn, would you say a few words before we each give Thad a personal farewell?"

"It would be my honor," Fawn said. "Cheri, Sarah, Jonathon, Michael, Ben, Samuel, you have chosen a perfect place to send off Thad. You call this mountaintop Sahalie, but there are many Sahalies in this world. It is a word that means 'high, holy place' and I can feel the essence of my ancestors here.

"This is a place close to the spirit world, a place where our bodies no longer matter, where only our deeds matter. Thad has taken leave of his body, and so we now send it forth to nurture new life and new deeds," Fawn finished and bowed with her cupped hands held forth. The others followed her example.

With a smile that revealed the certainty that her late husband, her soul mate, was at her side, thanking her for fulfilling his last request, Cheri told them, "Please take

Thad where you will, say a last goodbye and release him to this place he so loved."

Samuel stood uncertainly for a moment while the others all moved off to scatter Thad's ashes. In which direction would Thad want him to spread the ashes? West? North? South? East?

He closed his eyes hoping for inspiration. He received it in the form of a tap on his wrist. Opening his eyes, Sarah stood at his side. "Can I join you? I'm a little flustered by all this. I'm not sure what Thad would want me to do."

"Me either," Samuel admitted. "Maybe west? That's where the sun's heading."

"Yeah, Thad would like that," Sarah said softly.

Carefully, with cradled hands, they moved to the west side of the summit where the craggy crown of the mountaintop fractured into three broad outcroppings. Samuel stepped up onto a broad swath of rock directly aligned with the sun.

"How about here?" he asked.

She fixed her gaze on the rugged expanse of peaks and valleys stretching out beyond Samuel. She smiled serenely, and with a graceful step, joined him. They stood side by side.

Sarah raised her cupped palms as tears streamed down her cheeks. She closed her eyes for a moment, and then opened them as she offered up her palms to the setting sun. A sudden gust of wind lifted Thad's ashes up and out into the open space beneath her. Sarah mouthed a final message only Thad could hear.

Samuel said a silent goodbye to his friend, the Elder, opening his hands a moment after Sarah. The dust swept over his fingertips and flew beyond Sahalie into the primal heart of the Cascade Mountains.

Thad's sudden death had taken Samuel to the edge, pushing him to look closely at his life...and his future. To discover the value in the way his best friend had lived his life and had prepared himself for death. He'd created a legacy of giving and joy in those around him. Samuel knew that, someday, he would join Thad in that inescapable final journey all humans face. But first, before he reached his own end, he would explore the trail his best friend had blazed for him as an Elder.

He turned to face Sarah and serenely took the first step toward making the rest of his life the best of his life.

-The Beginning-

AFTERWORD

THIS FABLE IS THE FIRST IN A SERIES ABOUT growing older with purpose and mastery.

We are all growing older. We may have names for each 'new' generation. We may talk about a 'generation gap.' But fundamentally, we are all connected. We are one global family, living interdependently on one planet. And today, more than ever, we need what Elders can offer to our collective future: their unique perspective and their wisdom.

Elders can help us see ourselves, our relationships to others and what's happening in the world. They can see connections between disparate things that we cannot. They can help us create new possibilities. And they can create a 'new' story about aging that we can live into. A story in which we can continue to grow and experience well-being, happiness, satisfaction and fulfillment until our last day.

Becoming an Elder is a choice.

Samuel has made that choice. His journey is just beginning. Eldering has given him new purpose. Becoming an Elder is the next step.

You too can begin to put your wisdom into action and create a more positive future for yourself and those you love. Perhaps even a more positive future for humanity.

The choice is yours.

We hope you'll join us.

Visit us at TheElder.org to learn more about our programs and updates on THE ELDER series.

DR. MARC B. COOPER

Principal
The Eldering Institute

DR. COOPER has a wealth of experience to draw on as an Elder. His professional career includes academician, medical researcher, teacher, trainer, board director, inventor and entrepreneur. He has authored five books and writes a weekly newsletter with subscribers in more than 30 countries.

Marc is no stranger to major transitions and lifelong learning. After obtaining degrees in dentistry, periodontics and immunology and owning a dental practice for 14 years, he changed careers to become a consultant and coach. In 1984, drawing on his studies in various disciplines and his work as an independent contractor with several top consulting companies, he founded *The Mastery Company* to serve the healthcare and medical industries. He has since worked with large hospital systems, Silicon Valley start-ups, Fortune 500s and innumerable solo private practices to transform their businesses. Dr. Cooper has active clients in the US, Canada, Europe and the United Arab Emirates.

For the past decade, Marc's commitment to helping people live their lives with mastery and purpose—at any age—has led him to explore 'eldering.' He has facilitated engagements with hospice centers in major hospitals, trained with Rabbi Zalman Schacter-Shalomi (*Aging to Sage-ing*), and been involved with Elders of the Taos Pueblo in northern New Mexico.

JAMES C. SELMAN

Founder

The Eldering Institute

JAMES (JIM) SELMAN has been involved in the field of personal and organizational transformation since 1975. His interest in aging began in 1980 when, as the youngest member of the California Commission on Aging, he asserted that most of our attitudes and experience of aging are based on 'cultural stories.' When we change our story, we can transform how we relate to the future and how we experience age. In 1981, he founded *Growing Older, Inc.*, a not-for-profit organization with a mission to ensure that the last day of life holds as much possibility as the first.

In the past five years, he has come to appreciate that age is one of the most fundamental factors affecting how we experience our day-to-day lives, the possibilities we have and how we relate to ourselves, our circumstances and other people.

As an Elder, Jim is widely recognized as a pioneer and innovative leader in bringing about culture change in corporations and communities in the United States, Canada, South America and Europe.

Jim continues to demonstrate his wisdom in action by working with clients through his company *Paracomm Partners International*, mentoring aspiring young leaders, and sharing his wisdom and perspective—the gifts of his age—with consultants and organizations committed to making the world work for everyone.

LaVergne, TN USA
29 March 2011
222067LV00012B/105/P